FROM FAMINE

TO

FULLNESS

THE GOSPEL ACCORDING TO
THE OLD TESTAMENT

A series of studies on the lives
of Old Testament characters, written for
laypeople and pastors, and designed to
encourage Christ-centered reading, teaching,
and preaching of the Old Testament

TREMPER LONGMAN III
J. ALAN GROVES

Series Editors

FROM FAMINE

TO

FULLNESS

THE GOSPEL ACCORDING TO

RUTH

DEAN R. ULRICH

P&R
PUBLISHING
P.O. BOX 817 • PHILLIPSBURG • NEW JERSEY 08865-0817

Page design by Tobias Design

Printed in the United States of America

Library of Congress Cataloging-in-Publication Data

Ulrich, Dean R., 1963–
From famine to fullness : the Gospel according to Ruth / Dean R. Ulrich.
    p. cm. — (The Gospel according to the Old Testament)
Includes bibliographical references (p. 169) and index.
ISBN-13: 978-1-59638-009-7 (pbk.)
1. Bible. O.T. Ruth—Criticism, interpretation, etc. I. Title.
BS1315.52.U47 2007
222'.3506—dc22
                                        2007026232

To Arthur and Karen Schwab

with gratitude

CONTENTS

FOREWORD

The New Testament is in the Old concealed;
the Old Testament is in the New revealed.
—Augustine

Concerning this salvation, the prophets, who spoke of the grace that was to come to you, searched intently and with the greatest care, trying to find out the time and circumstances to which the Spirit of Christ in them was pointing when he predicted the sufferings of Christ and the glories that would follow. It was revealed to them that they were not serving themselves but you, when they spoke of the things that have now been told you by those who have preached the gospel to you by the Holy Spirit sent from heaven. Even angels long to look into these things. (1 Peter 1:10–12)

"In addition, some of our women amazed us. They went to the tomb early this morning but didn't find his body. They came and told us that they had seen a vision of angels, who said he was alive. Then some of our companions went to the tomb and found it just as the women had said, but him they did not see." He said to them, "How foolish you are, and how slow of heart to believe all that the prophets have spoken! Did not the Christ have to suffer these things and then enter his glory?" And beginning with Moses and all the Prophets, he explained to them what was said in all the Scriptures concerning himself. (Luke 24:22–27)

The prophets searched. Angels longed to see. And the disciples didn't understand. But Moses, the prophets, and all the Old Testament Scriptures had spoken about it—that Jesus would come, suffer, and then be glorified. God began to tell a story in the Old Testament, the ending of which the audience eagerly anticipated. But the Old Testament audience was left hanging. The plot was laid out but the climax was delayed. The unfinished story begged an ending. In Christ, God has provided the climax to the Old Testament story. Jesus did not arrive unannounced; his coming was declared *in advance* in the Old Testament, not just in explicit prophecies of the Messiah but by means of the stories of all of the events, characters, and circumstances in the Old Testament. God was telling a larger, overarching, unified story. From the account of creation in Genesis to the final stories of the return from exile, God progressively unfolded his plan of salvation. And the Old Testament account of that plan always pointed in some way to Christ.

AIMS OF THIS SERIES

The Gospel According to the Old Testament Series is committed to the proposition that the Bible, both Old and New Testaments, is a unified revelation of God, and that its thematic unity is found in Christ. The individual books of the Old Testament exhibit diverse genres, styles, and individual theologies, but tying them all together is the constant foreshadowing of, and pointing forward to, Christ. Believing in the fundamentally Christocentric nature of the Old Testament, as well as the New Testament, we offer this series of studies in the Old Testament with the following aims:

- to lay out the pervasiveness of the revelation of Christ in the Old Testament
- to promote a Christ-centered reading of the Old Testament
- to encourage Christ-centered preaching and teaching from the Old Testament

To this end, the volumes in this series are written for pastors and laypeople, not scholars.

While such a series could take a number of different shapes, we have decided, in most cases, to focus individual volumes on Old Testament figures—people—rather than books or themes. Some books, of course, will receive major attention in connection with their authors or main characters (e.g., Daniel or Isaiah). Also, certain themes will be emphasized in connection with particular figures.

It is our hope and prayer that this series will revive interest in and study of the Old Testament as readers recognize that the Old Testament points forward to Jesus Christ.

TREMPER LONGMAN III
J. ALAN GROVES

ACKNOWLEDGMENTS

A t one level of reading, the book of Ruth demonstrates how people of faith help one another and so promote the advancement of God's kingdom in their midst. This book on Ruth attests to the investment and sacrifice that several dear saints have made on my behalf. I wish to acknowledge and thank them now.

I begin with my wife, Dawn, who has supported my academic and pastoral callings throughout our marriage. She has modeled the faith and faithfulness of Ruth and so made our marriage a blessing to me as well as to others. She believed that I had something to say on the Old Testament, even when I was not so sure. I would be remiss if I did not thank our children, Cindy and Gordon, for continually reminding me that there is more to life than reading and writing theological scholarship. Their zest for activity has provided needed opportunities for me to clear my head when I was unsure of what to say next.

I thank my parents, Rich and Ann Ulrich, for raising me in a godly home and giving abundantly of their resources for my education. I also acknowledge my mother-in-law, Celia Errickson, for her support of my wife and me during the early years of our marriage as I moved through my doctoral program. I regret that neither my father nor my mother-in-law lived long enough to see the publication of this book.

I thank the editors of this series, Tremper Longman III and Alan Groves, for helping me complete this project. Their assistance actually began years ago when I had the privilege of studying under them at Westminster Theological Seminary. Their mastery of the Old Testament, especially a redemptive-historical approach to it, has profoundly affected my teaching and preaching. In this regard, I fondly remember their former colleague and my professor, Raymond Dillard, who contributed the first volume to the Gospel According to the Old Testament Series. While this book was with the publisher, Alan Groves lost his bout with cancer on February 5, 2007. Especially by means of a blogsite, he and his wife, Libby, have appreciably offered an eloquent and transparent testimony to their trust in the God under whose wings they, like Ruth, have taken refuge.

My thanks also go to Jeremy Keiper and Jim Krizan of the Information Technology Department of Trinity Episcopal School for Ministry. Jeremy and Jim helped me discover some of the formatting intricacies of Microsoft Word. They took me to screens that I had never before seen. Eric Anest of P&R picked up where Jeremy and Jim left off and transformed a manuscript into a book. I express my gratitude to him and others at P&R.

This book began as a series of sermons and adult education lessons at Christ Presbyterian Church (PCA) in Chippewa, Pennsylvania; Church of the Ascension (Episcopal) in Oakland, Pennsylvania; and Covenant Community Presbyterian Church (PCA) in Wexford, Pennsylvania. My thanks go to the members of those churches who graciously listened to my initial attempts to think through the message and application of Ruth.

Lastly, I take this opportunity to acknowledge the great benevolence of Arthur and Karen Schwab. Without their generosity, I may not have obtained the advanced education necessary to write this book or prepare seminarians to preach the Old Testament. I can never repay the debt of gratitude that is owed them, but dedicating this book to them is my latest attempt. Art and Karen, I thank you.

ABBREVIATIONS

AB	Anchor Bible
BibInt	*Biblical Interpretation*
BJS	Brown Judaic Studies
BSac	*Bibliotheca Sacra*
HBT	*Horizons in Biblical Theology*
HUCA	*Hebrew Union College Annual*
Int	*Interpretation*
JBL	*Journal of Biblical Literature*
JETS	*Journal of the Evangelical Theological Society*
JSOT	*Journal for the Study of the Old Testament*
Jsotsup	JSOT Supplement Series
NAC	New American Commentary
NICOT	New International Commentary on the Old Testament
NIVAC	NIV Application Commentary
TynBul	*Tyndale Bulletin*
VT	*Vetus Testamentum*
WBC	Word Biblical Commentary
WTJ	*Westminster Theological Journal*

PREFACE

It is fair to say that most readers of the Bible enjoy the book of Ruth. As I have preached and taught this book, people from a variety of backgrounds have been drawn to it. Their ears have perked up when they heard, "Please turn to the book of Ruth." Why is this, though? Several possibilities come to mind.

Maybe people thrill to the love story of Ruth and Boaz. More than a few years ago, a popular song artist observed, "Some people want to fill the world with silly love songs." He then asked, "Well, what's wrong with that? I need to know 'cause here I go again." As a race, we humans cannot seem to get our fill of songs and stories about love, and the book of Ruth in popular and scholarly estimation certainly takes its place among the best of love stories. In this book, true love triumphs over multiple forms of adversity and brings good to all who are touched by it. How many such songs and stories does the human race need? The sheer volume of those written would suggest that we cannot get enough love songs and stories. Moreover, we listen to and read the "oldies but goodies" again and again.

Readers of Ruth may also find hope and encouragement in the happy ending for Naomi. Who cannot, to some extent or another, identify with this older woman who has been battered by life's relentless storms and bruised by its painful memories? Who has not wondered with Naomi where God is in the midst of deprivation and loss or even considered the unthinkable option that "the Almighty has brought misfortune upon me" (Ruth 1:21)? No one dispassionately reads the book of Ruth to get a glimpse of how "the other side lives" or to make an academic study of human suffering. The book of Ruth tells everyone's story, even your story, about the hardships of life. Though the book of Ruth is set in the ancient days of the judges, the hardships that its characters face transcend time and culture. In the midst of our own headaches and heartaches, we need stories such as Ruth that end well, for these help us look beyond our troubles and disappointments to a brighter future. The realized hope of others offers perspective for us, who in our own way can relate to the setbacks described in the opening verses of Ruth.

Yet another attraction to the book of Ruth is the positive traits of its characters, especially Ruth and Boaz. Readers of the book of Ruth cannot help but admire Ruth's unquenchable loyalty to her mother-in-law or Boaz's extraordinary compassion toward two destitute widows, one of whom was a foreigner. Loyalty and compassion—these are qualities that receive separate sections in William Bennett's highly regarded *The Book of Virtues*. Adults value these qualities in themselves, and parents try to inculcate them in their children. Bennett's book even contains a paraphrase of the book of Ruth, though it is placed in the section devoted to the virtue of friendship. By way of introduction to this paraphrase, Bennett says, "Ruth's words to Naomi [in Ruth 1:16–17] are one of the greatest statements of friendship and loyalty in all of literature."[1] Yes they are, and Ruth and Boaz certainly stand out as exemplars of certain moral virtues.

From a literary point of view, then, the book of Ruth ranks as a good story. It surely warms the heart in more than one way and challenges its readers with ideals that are universally esteemed. It is understandable that readers of Ruth would enjoy this literary masterpiece and repeatedly turn to it for inspiration.

Some readers, though, may question the subtitle of my book. Indeed, as the title suggests, the book of Ruth moves from famine at the beginning to fullness in the form of the provision of food in the middle and the birth of an heir at the end. But can I appropriately refer to the gospel according to the book of Ruth? Perhaps this subtitle claims too much by inferring that the book of Ruth is more than a human-interest story that instructs its readers to be morally virtuous like Ruth and Boaz. Where is the gospel—the good news of salvation from sin—in this quaint and heart-warming Old Testament story? Where is the Savior, Jesus Christ, in a short story that never mentions his name? Surely, one cannot seriously read such a nostalgic tale as part of the grand, sweeping story of God's plan of redemption that reaches its climax in the incarnation of his Son.

For the last century or so, biblical scholars have been inclined to agree that the book of Ruth has little, if anything, to do with the gospel of Jesus Christ. This is so because of two stages in the history of interpreting Ruth. The first stage is suggested by Ronald Hals in his *The Theology of the Book of Ruth* that appeared in 1969.[2] Until that time, scholars as a rule doubted that the book of Ruth was a work of theology, that is, a book that taught about God's saving activity. Instead, they considered the book of Ruth a charming and idyllic tale about humans who persevered against great odds in a bleak time and survived. By contrast, Hals argued that the book of Ruth utilizes a narrative form to teach about the doctrine of God's providence. In the years since 1969, an increasing number of scholars have questioned whether the book of Ruth is such a charming story after all. Feminist scholars particularly notice the seemingly hopeless predicament of Naomi, Orpah, and Ruth and inveigh against the inequity, oppression, and destitution that result, in their estimation, from patriarchy. Boaz, then, is not considered heroic; rather, he is part of the ongoing problem of women's economic dependence on male provision. Nevertheless, feminist readers maintain that the book of Ruth, despite its traces of androcentrism, illustrates how women who take initiative for their own well-being can bring about favorable changes of fortune and secure their place in society without male patronage.[3] For different reasons, then, the pre-1969 and post-1969 stages of interpreting Ruth have downplayed, even ignored, recognition of the gospel message of this biblical book.

My reading of Ruth, however, presupposes that the book of Ruth, whatever it might say about humans who persevere or women who take initiative, has a theological message rooted in God's oversight of the movement of redemptive history that climaxes in the person and work of Jesus Christ. In Luke 24, no less an interpreter of the Old Testament than Jesus told his disciples (and us) that the authors of the Old Testament wrote about him:

He [Jesus] said to them [the two men on the road to Emmaus], "How foolish you are, and how slow of heart to believe all that the prophets have spoken! Did not the Christ have to suffer these things and then enter his glory?" And beginning with Moses and all the Prophets, he explained to them what was said in all the Scriptures concerning himself. (Luke 24:25–27)

He [Jesus] said to them [the eleven disciples], "This is what I told you while I was still with you: Everything must be fulfilled that is written about me in the Law of Moses, the Prophets and the Psalms." (Luke 24:44)

Evangelical scholars routinely understand Moses, the Prophets, and the Psalms to refer to the tripartite division of the Old Testament canon into the Law, the Prophets, and the Writings. In other words, Jesus said that the whole Old Testament, of which Ruth is a part, bears witness to him as the Savior who suffers for the salvation of his people. Hence, the book of Ruth as part of the Old Testament canon is rightly read as a contribution to the unfolding plan of God to redeem his fallen creation from sin and its deleterious effects. The struggle to survive and the bias against women may be two of those regrettable effects, but it is the gospel of Jesus Christ that takes care of the sin problem in the human heart and brings about the transformation of character, conduct, and consequences.

This redemptive-historical approach to interpreting the book of Ruth inevitably affects one's study of the major characters, especially Ruth and Boaz. The human characters are, of course, involved in the story, but they are not what the book is foremost about. They do not appear for their own sake; hence, the book of Ruth is not a biography. God—not Naomi, Ruth, or Boaz—is the main character, and he works through the human characters to advance his sovereign and redemptive purpose.[4] While it is true that God is concerned about moral and virtuous conduct, which Ruth and Boaz exhibit, such conduct is not possible apart from a relationship with God that he sovereignly and graciously establishes through covenant. For this reason, the message of the book of Ruth is not simply "Be like Ruth and Boaz." Fallen humans cannot be like Ruth and Boaz unless they are in relationship with the God of Ruth and Boaz. Such a relationship was proleptically possible for Ruth and Boaz under the old covenant, for the old covenant anticipated the new covenant in Jesus Christ. Faith in Jesus Christ makes relationship with God possible, and such faith transforms one's character and conduct so that believers respond to the situations of their lives with a desire and intention to do God's will for God's glory.[5]

Ruth and Boaz were certainly people of faith and as such models of good conduct. As evidenced by the moral imperatives throughout the Bible and by Paul's reference to events in the books of Exodus and Numbers that provided examples for the Corinthians (1 Cor. 10:1–11), God does want his people to lead upright lives that conform to his revealed moral standards. Still, the modern believer does not aspire to be like Ruth and Boaz for the sake of being moral and virtuous. Morality and virtue are not the "chief end of man," to borrow language from the Westminster Shorter Catechism. They are the result of God's grace through Jesus Christ and part of the good work that God has foreordained for his people to do for the advancement of Christ's kingdom and the glory of God. If God's grace is the prerequisite for being like Ruth and Boaz, then our obedient response to God's grace in the situations of life, that is, being like Ruth and Boaz, brings glory to God. This is our chief end.

Ultimately, then, the book of Ruth is a profound account of God's providence in the lives of otherwise ordinary people who observed God's covenant in rather mundane circumstances. As we shall see in the chapters that follow, what God does through the faithfulness of Ruth and Boaz is nothing short of stunning. Because the God of Naomi, Ruth, and Boaz is also our God, we similarly can expect him to perform great and mighty deeds that advance his glorious purpose of reconciling all things to his eternal plan.

I

IT WAS NOT
THE BEST OF TIMES

Charles Dickens began *A Tale of Two Cities* with the well-known words: "It was the best of times, it was the worst of times." The book of Ruth opens with a reference to the days when the judges ruled. With that recollection of the people and events described in the book of Judges, the author of Ruth informed his or her audience that the historical, social, and religious context for what follows was not the best of times. In fact, the dark days of the judges were closer to the worst of times in Old Testament history. Elimelech and his wife Naomi, whom the reader meets in the opening verses, lived during a time of apostasy, injustice, and tumult.

This chapter aims to set the book of Ruth in its larger context, both historically and religiously. Familiarity with the days of the judges will increase our appreciation for the godliness of Ruth and Boaz and, more importantly, for the gracious and providential activity of God in the lives of Naomi, Ruth, and Boaz. Before discussing the period of the judges, let us briefly review Old Testament history to this point. We shall start with Abraham.

FROM ABRAHAM TO THE JUDGES

For our purpose, we can say that Abraham lived about 2000 B.C. God made a covenant with him and directed him to relocate from Ur to Canaan by way of Haran. Although God promised to bless the nations through the descendants of Abraham, Abraham and his descendants seemed, more often than not, to be at odds with their neighbors or at least at their mercy. As it had Abraham (Gen. 12:10), famine drove Abraham's grandson, Jacob, and his family to Egypt for food. While in Egypt, Jacob's descendants multiplied and experienced oppression because of the perceived threat that their increasing number posed to the pharaoh. If the biblical chronology (cf. Ex. 12:40; Deut. 1:3; 1 Kings 6:1) is taken at face value, Jacob went to Egypt about 1876 B.C.; the exodus occurred about 1446 B.C.; and the conquest began about 1406 B.C.[1] Joshua and Caleb were the only members of the exodus generation to live through the wilderness years and participate in the possession of the Promised Land. All other members of the exodus generation died in the wilderness because of their unbelief—in particular, their fearful and disobedient response to the report of the spies (Num. 13). As seen in Numbers 26–36, the children of the exodus generation received a fresh start and an open future. The book of Joshua reports that they did not shrink back from the promises and commands of God but followed the lead of Joshua, the Lord's appointed successor to Moses. After the major campaigns of the conquest, Joshua, Caleb, and the children of the exodus generation reached the end of their earthly lives. The judges period commenced with the grandchildren of the exodus generation.

At the time of the exodus, Egypt and Hatti (in eastern Turkey) vied for control of Canaan, especially its trade routes and seaports. By the middle of the thirteenth century, Egypt and Hatti had grown weary of war, and they sealed a peace agreement through a royal marriage. The Egyptian pharaoh, Rameses II, married the daughter of the Hittite king, Hattusilis. Canaan reverted to Egyptian oversight, but the dust did not remain settled for long. The migration of the Philistines to Canaan from points west at the end of the thirteenth century put an end to the Hittite kingdom and once again turned Canaan into a political football until the reign of David about 1000 B.C. Israel then reached the zenith of its political stability, power, and influence during the years of David and Solomon—even becoming a major force in the ancient Near East. The observation to be made now is that the events of the book of Ruth took place at a time in ancient Near Eastern history when no nation was the undisputed superpower of the day. The instability among the tribes during the judges period mirrored the flux and turbulence among other peoples.

The book of Joshua records the Israelite conquest of Canaan in which the army of Israel served as God's penal agent to mete out punishment for the immorality of the Canaanites. The Pentateuch anticipates this penal role that the descendants of Abraham would play:

> In the fourth generation your [Abraham's] descendants will come back here, for the sin of the Amorites has not yet reached its full measure. (Gen. 15:16)

> You must not do as they do in Egypt, where you used to live, and you must not do as they do in the land of Canaan, where I am bringing you. Do not follow their practices. . . . Do not defile yourselves in any of these ways, because this is how the nations that I am going to drive out before you became defiled. Even the land was defiled; so I punished it for its sin, and the land vomited out its inhabitants. (Lev. 18:3, 24–25)

You [Moses] and Aaron are to number by their divisions all the men in Israel twenty years old or more who are able to serve in the army. (Num. 1:3)

When the LORD your God brings you into the land you are entering to possess and drives out before you many nations—the Hittites, Girgashites, Amorites, Canaanites, Perizzites, Hivites and Jebusites, seven nations larger and stronger than you—and when the LORD your God has delivered them over to you and you have defeated them, then you must destroy them totally. Make no treaty with them and show them no mercy. (Deut. 7:1–2)

After the LORD your God has driven them out before you, do not say to yourself, "The LORD has brought me here to take possession of this land because of my righteousness." No, it is on account of the wickedness of these nations that the LORD is going to drive them out before you. It is not because of your righteousness or your integrity that you are going in to take possession of their land; but on account of the wickedness of these nations, the LORD your God will drive them out before you, to accomplish what he swore to your fathers, to Abraham, Isaac and Jacob. Understand, then, that it is not because of your righteousness that the LORD your God is giving you this good land to possess, for you are a stiff-necked people. (Deut. 9:4–6)

Taking all these passages together, readers may conclude that the wars in Joshua cannot be assigned an imperialistic motive on the part of a group of escapees in search of living space. Yahweh used the Israelites to punish the Canaanites, even as he later used other nations to punish Israel and Judah. Deuteronomy 9 is up front about the reality that the Israelites were not morally superior to the Canaanites. God was using one group of sinful people to accomplish his purpose for another group of sinful people. Ultimately what Israel did as a holy army against the Canaanites promoted its role as a kingdom of priests among the rest of the nations.

Joshua 1–12 describes the three decisive strikes against the central, southern, and northern Canaanites. Two verses recall the penal purpose of Israel's aggression. The first has to do with the Gibeonite ruse:

> They [the Gibeonites] answered Joshua, "Your servants were clearly told how the LORD your God had commanded his servant Moses to give you the whole land and to wipe out all its inhabitants from before you. So we feared for our lives because of you, and that is why we did this." (Josh. 9:24)

The second serves as a summary of the three strikes:

> For it was the LORD himself who hardened their hearts to wage war against Israel, so that he might destroy them totally, exterminating them without mercy, as the LORD had commanded Moses. (Josh. 11:20)

After these campaigns, it was evident that Israel was in the land to stay. Yahweh had kept his promise and given his people what seemed to be, from a human point of view, an unlikely victory against superior forces.

Joshua 13, however, indicates that the fighting had not yet ended, for each tribe had to mop up its patrimony by eliminating Canaanite enclaves that survived the initial strikes. Judges 1 makes the same point. It might be helpful to think of Joshua in terms of D-day and V-day of World War II. If D-day constituted the decisive strike (in Europe) and V-day marked the end of the fighting (whether in Europe or the Pacific), then Joshua 12 looks back at D-day, and Joshua 13–Judges 1 anticipates V-day.

The same analogy holds true for God's people who live between the two comings of Jesus Christ. If the cross and resurrection of Jesus represent the decisive strike against sin, death, and Satan, the second coming corresponds to V-day. At that time, God's holy war against all that opposes his plan to exalt his Son will end in triumph. In the words of Paul, "every knee [will] bow . . . and every tongue confess that Jesus Christ is Lord, to the glory of God the Father" (Phil. 2:10–11). Between the two comings of Jesus, believers experience what is often called the tension between the already and the not yet. Jesus' followers can look back and see that D-day, the decisive strike, has already occurred and now guarantees thorough defeat of the enemy. Nevertheless, the time after the first coming and before the second coming involves ongoing warfare with the spiritual forces of darkness and their terrestrial supporters. V-day has not yet arrived, and so the potential for setbacks and defeats still exists. All too often, God's people succumb to temptation and score a victory for the enemies of God. Still, the decisive strike at the first coming of Jesus guarantees ultimate victory at the second, and Jesus' followers fight the good fight with assurance that God who has begun a good work at the first coming of Jesus will bring it to completion at the second.

THE BOOK OF JUDGES ON
THE DAYS OF THE JUDGES

As seen in Judges, though, V-day never came for the children or grandchildren of the exodus generation. The book of Judges divides into three sections, and each section describes the fight against the enemies of God. All three sections present the failure of God's people at that time to secure a final and definitive victory over the enemy. It should be noted that the books of Samuel present David as the one who finished the conquest, but even this observation, as will be seen later, requires some nuancing.

The first section of Judges (1:1–3:6) summarizes the period of the judges, making the observation that the generation after Joshua (i.e., the grandchildren of the exodus generation and following) did not keep faith with their covenant God. Due to lapses in faith and obedience, they failed to finish the conquest and allowed the Canaanite pockets of resistance to remain and regroup. For the tribes, living among the Canaanites soon led to worshiping with them—the concern of Deuteronomy 20:17–18:

> Completely destroy them—the Hittites, Amorites, Canaanites, Perizzites, Hivites and Jebusites—as the LORD your God has commanded you. Otherwise, they will teach you to follow all the detestable things they do in worshiping their gods, and you will sin against the LORD your God.

What began as complacency and tolerance became apostasy. In his study of Judges, Dale Ralph Davis used the expression "generation degeneration," which certainly captures the point that this first section of Judges is trying to make.[2]

The second section, Judges 3:7–16:31, shows how things went from bad to worse, especially among the leaders. While the thirteen judges who are mentioned in the book of Judges probably overlapped one another to some extent, the order of their appearance in Judges seems to have intentional movement. The judges, as they are "brought on stage" in the book, become less admirable and effective. Othniel, the first judge described, represents the ideal about whom nothing negative is said. In the power of God's Spirit, Othniel delivered God's people from the hand of Cushan-Rishathaim of Aram Naharaim. The play on words goes beyond assonance to the meanings of the names. The king's name means "dark and doubly wicked," and Mr. Dark and Doubly Wicked comes from the land of two rivers.[3] The point is that the first judge, like his father-in-law Caleb, relied on God to overcome a formidable adversary.

Gideon, the fifth judge described, was a mixed bag of virtue and vice. The mighty warrior who won a stunning victory with only three hundred troops also hesitated to heed God's command and made an unauthorized ephod that became an idolatrous snare. Gideon embodied the religious schizophrenia of the people whom he delivered from the Midianites. As for Samson, the thirteenth judge, not much good can be said about him. The judge who wanted to live with the Philistines also died with them, seeking not the advancement of God's plan for his people but only revenge for the loss of his eyes. Especially at his death, Samson may have checked the Philistine hegemony over Israel and so been used of God to preserve Israel as a sociopolitical entity, but the book of Judges never indicates that Samson promoted faithfulness to the covenant. While Deborah, the fourth judge described, is arguably the most honorable person in the book, her role as judge is troubling. Why were the men so weak-willed, and what would happen when there was no Deborah, only a Delilah? Deborah was not so much a picture of the way things ought to be as she was a testimony to the way things were, and in the days of the judges, things were definitely not the way they were supposed to be. Rather, the tribes of Israel succumbed more and more to Canaanite culture and religion.

The third section, Judges 17–21, describes the eventual disintegration of Israelite society. Moral chaos prevailed among the people who were supposed to model a redeemed society to the rest of the world. These chapters put much of the blame on the Levites, who neither obeyed God's commands to them as religious leaders nor taught God's law to the laity among the tribes. Because of the resulting ignorance and disregard of the law, many people were hurt, and what happened to women is more than most modern readers can stomach. If a society can be judged by how it treats its women and children, then Israelite society during the days of the judges had lost all sense of decency, justice, commitment, and protection. In short, it had forgotten how to love.

Even so, the book of Judges does more than describe a people that are sick unto death. It also hints at better days to come. Throughout the third section (17:6; 18:1; 19:1; 21:25), a refrain repeatedly puts forth monarchy as the solution to moral chaos: "In those days Israel had no king; everyone did as he saw fit." Because the writer of Judges believed that anarchy prevails in the absence of a king, the book of Judges, especially chapters 17–21, prepares the reader for kingship. But not just any king will suffice, for a subtle debate about the right king runs below the surface. The contestants are Saul and David, and the writer of Judges indirectly threw his or her support behind David. This is seen in several ways.

First, David's tribe, Judah, receives priority at two places toward the beginning and end of the book. In Judges 1:2 Yahweh commanded Judah to lead the other tribes in the mop-up operation against the remaining Canaanites, and then in 20:18 Yahweh again ordered Judah to take the lead in the civil war over the unseemly incident that ended in the death of a Levite's concubine. In both cases Saul's tribe, Benjamin, was said by the writer of Judges to bear responsibility for a failure to do God's will. In Judges 1:21 the Benjamites were unable to finish the conquest against the Jebusites who lived in Jerusalem.[4] In chapters 19–20 the men of Gibeah in Benjamin wanted to have homosexual relations with a Levite and instead raped his concubine to the point of death. When confronted with this sin in their midst, the rest of the men of Benjamin refused to redress the wrong by either punishing the men of Gibeah themselves or handing the men of Gibeah over to the other tribes. Given the degree of lawlessness in Benjamin, who would want a king from there?

Second, the account of Abimelech in Judges 9 reminds its readers of two less than flattering facts about Saul's reign. The first of these is found in Judges 9:23, which reports that Yahweh sent an evil spirit between Abimelech and the citizens of Shechem. The reason had to do with Abimelech's earlier elimination of his seventy brothers who all had Gideon as their father. Judges 9:24 indicates that both Abimelech and the citizens of Shechem had a hand in the killings. It is profitable to know that Abimelech's name means "My father is king." While Gideon outwardly and piously refused an invitation to become king (Judg. 8:23), he nevertheless acted as a king by amassing wealth and wives—both of which were proscribed by the deuteronomic regulations for kingship (Deut. 17:17). The point is that neither Gideon nor Abimelech was the right kind of king for whom the author of Judges was looking. Of course, Yahweh later sent an evil spirit to trouble Saul who similarly had demonstrated that he was not the right man to lead God's people in faithfulness to God's covenant (1 Sam. 16:14). The second comparison between Abimelech and Saul concerns their deaths. According to Judges 9:54 and 1 Samuel 31:4, both Abimelech and Saul sustained wounds in battle and ordered their armor-bearers to finish them with their own swords. So far as the writer of Judges was concerned, Abimelech and Saul were royal pretenders who met an expected demise.

Third, Jephthah made a rash vow in the context of battle against Ammon (Judg. 11:30–31). If God gave him victory, he would sacrifice whatever met him at the door of his house when he returned. That vow cost Jephthah's daughter her life, for she was the first to greet him. Saul similarly made a foolish vow that nearly resulted in the death of his son Jonathan (1 Sam. 14:24). Saul irrationally forbade his troops to eat before triumphing in battle against the Philistines. Meanwhile, Jonathan almost single-handedly defeated the Philistines and was unaware of his father's oath. Exhausted from his efforts, Jonathan innocently ate some wild honey and would have been put to death by Saul if the troops had not intervened on his behalf.

Fourth, Judges 19 reports that the Levite and his concubine stayed in two places and received opposite treatment. They lodged first in Bethlehem, David's hometown, and received not one but four nights of generous room and board. They lodged second in Gibeah, Saul's hometown, where no one offered them anything until an old farmer came home from the field. But then the other men of Gibeah interrupted the old farmer's kindness by demanding to sodomize his male guest. Eventually, they raped and killed his female guest. The original readers would not miss the political implications: the king from Bethlehem (David) would treat them better than would the king from Gibeah (Saul).

Fifth, Judges 19:29 reports the Levite's gruesome cutting of his concubine's lifeless body into twelve parts that were then distributed among the tribes. He did this to draw attention to the Benjamites' disregard of moral decency. Similarly, Saul cut two oxen into pieces and sent them throughout Israel to alert the tribes to Ammonite cruelty among the residents of Jabesh Gilead (1 Sam. 11:7). The Ammonites had invaded Jabesh Gilead, and the terms of surrender required the men of Jabesh Gilead to gouge out their right eyes.

The books of Judges and 1 Samuel have a number of parallels between the judges period and Saul's reign. Because the original readers of Judges were familiar with Saul's reign, they would have recognized these parallels and understood that Judges as a whole is a polemic against Saul and an apology for David. Marc Zvi Brettler says that the "allusions" to Saul in Judges "all function in the same way—they make Saul look bad."[5] The right king to quell the covenantal waywardness of the judges period was not Saul or his son Ish-Bosheth. Instead, the right king was David. The books of Samuel contend that Saul was the people's choice, a king according to their heart, whereas David was God's choice, a king according to God's heart. Through David and his descendants, God would redeem his people and fulfill his promises to Abraham.

What does all this have to do with the book of Ruth? Set in the period of the judges, the book of Ruth ends with the royal line of David and so names the king for which Judges is looking. In the midst of religious, moral, and societal collapse, God had not forgotten or withdrawn his redemptive plan. In all the apostasy and degeneracy, God was at work in the least likely circumstances and people to accomplish his purpose. Ruth gives hope when all hope seems lost.

Twenty-first-century readers should be able to identify with the period of the judges. Our contemporary thinkers and analysts say that we live in a postmodern age, but how similar are our times to the days of the judges when everyone did what was right in his or her own eyes? Postmodernism rejects the notion of absolute truth, universal norms, and ultimate coherence. In fact, it fears these because they allegedly represent a desire for power over others.[6] Perhaps with good reason, postmodernists distrust and reject the modernist affirmation of truth and morality. They have seen how the heirs of the Enlightenment program have used so-called natural law and self-evident truths to coerce and oppress. It nearly goes without saying, then, that postmodernism's aversion to absolute truth rules out any belief that humans are part of a metanarrative, a grand and sweeping story of God's creation and redemption. The existence of a transcendent and divine Playwright undermines the postmodern commitment to individually or communally defined meaning and morality. In short, postmodernism is about the autonomous self. Postmodernism affirms that there are as many stories as there are people or, better, communities of people. No story has a privileged place above the others; otherwise, there would be an objective and authoritative voice to which all other voices would have to submit.

But is the postmodern solution—everyone or every community doing what is right in his, her, or its eyes—feasible? Judges describes the oppressive and inhumane results of the autonomous self. In fact, unabashed and unbridled selfishness becomes every bit as horrifically injurious to others as authoritarianism is feared to be. The truth is that the postmodern reveling in chaos leads inevitably to tyranny. So teaches the book of 1 Samuel, which follows Judges in the Hebrew Bible and Ruth in English Bibles. It explains how a people living in moral chaos asked for a king like what the other nations had—a specialist in warfare. The lesson from Samuel's response to the request for a king (1 Sam. 8:10–18) is that moral chaos usually leads to tyranny because the latter is preferable to the former. Humans cannot live true to their autonomous yearnings. They may crave an unfettered lifestyle, but they soon willingly trade it for imposed order so as to escape the self-threatening consequences that follow from everyone else's lack of restraint. Both Judges and the books of Samuel suggest a different route to take. The answer to moral chaos is the right kind of king, God's choice.

Before the Israelites requested a king as described in 1 Samuel 8, Moses had anticipated that Israel would have a king after entering the land of Canaan. Deuteronomy 17:14–20 gives the regulations for kingship:

When you enter the land the LORD your God is giving you and have taken possession of it and settled in it, and you say, "Let us set a king over us like all the nations around us," be sure to appoint over you the king the LORD your God chooses. He must be from among your own brothers. Do not place a foreigner over you, one who is not a brother Israelite. The king, moreover, must not acquire great numbers of horses for himself or make the people return to Egypt to get more of them, for the LORD has told you, "You are not to go back that way again." He must not take many wives, or his heart will be led astray. He must not accumulate large amounts of silver and gold.

When he takes the throne of his kingdom, he is to write for himself on a scroll a copy of this law, taken from that of the priests, who are Levites. It is to be with him, and he is to read it all the days of his life so that he may learn to revere the LORD his God and follow carefully all the words of this law and these decrees and not consider himself better than his brothers and turn from the law to the right or to the left. Then he and his descendants will reign a long time over his kingdom in Israel.

God's people would need authority to hold them accountable to the revelation that they had received from Moses and would yet receive through prophets. The regulations for kingship in Deuteronomy 17 distinguished Israel's monarchs from their ancient Near Eastern counterparts. The former were supposed to promote and preserve adherence to God's revealed will in contrast to the latter, who enjoyed privileges at the expense of their subjects. In fact, a king of Israel upon being crowned was instructed to copy the law, presumably so that it might be fresh in his mind and readily accessible to him when a decision affecting God's people needed to be rendered. Though an Israelite king had authority over God's people, he was held to the same standard as they. Together, king and subjects would ideally model a God-fearing, Torah-keeping community to the surrounding Near Eastern peoples.

Judges may favor David as a covenantally minded king, but the books of Samuel nuance Judges. The books of Samuel are framed by Hannah's prayer in 1 Samuel 2 and David's song in 2 Samuel 22. Hannah's prayer repeats Judges' longing for the right kind of king, and David's song contains some of the same themes that were introduced by Hannah—for example, God as a rock, deliverance from enemies, protection of the faithful, humbling of the proud, victory for the anointed one. To some extent, the books of Samuel agree with Judges that David, not Saul, was the king of God's choice, but the books of Samuel also present a flawed David who did not fully answer Hannah's prayer. David may have been the Lord's anointed, but he was not the good shepherd who always cares for the sheep. One needs only to remember Uriah the husband of Bathsheba (2 Sam. 11). In fact, the books of Samuel end on a less than satisfying note as the royal shepherd, David, decided that the sheep would suffer for his sin of counting the troops (2 Sam. 24).[7] David and David's line may have been God's choice, but the books of Samuel look for a Davidic descendant who would be greater than David, even a Good Shepherd who would lay down his life for the sins of the sheep (cf. Zech. 11–13).

JUDGES AND THE GRACE OF GOD

By way of conclusion, the book of Judges ends on a pessimistic note. The whole book presents a people rotting at the core. From a covenantal perspective nothing is the way it is supposed to be—what Cornelius Plantinga calls a loss of *shalom*, the Hebrew word for "peace" or "whole-ness."[8] What is amazing at the end of Judges is that there is still an entity called Israel. Deuteronomy 28 promised blessing for obedience and curse for disobedience. Judges details the spiraling disobedience that would warrant the enactment of the curses and eventual severance of the covenantal relationship. For all the sin and judgment in Judges, however, grace also abounds. How often God inter-vened on Israel's behalf in spite of what it deserved. The tribes were determined to destroy themselves, but God would not allow it.[9] When Judges is read in view of the rest of the Bible, grace trumps justice but not at the denial of justice. God satisfied his own justice through the sacri-ficial system that pointed to the person and work of Jesus Christ, the Lamb of God who took away the sin of the world.

But why did God show grace? God had a mission for his people to be a kingdom of priests or a channel of redemptive blessing to the world. Any success in that mis-sion had less to do with the human participants and vir-tually everything to do with a covenant-keeping God. God would accomplish his redemptive purpose. Neither the gates of hell nor God's own people could stop him. At the end of Judges, God's promises remain in effect, but they are thrust into the future when there is a king in Israel. The books of Samuel and Kings, however, demonstrate that kingship brought its own infelicities and atrocities. The reader, then, must look for one who is greater than David and David's descendants, even Jesus Christ. How much brighter, though, God's grace in Christ shines against the blackness of the judges.

Ruth shows us that God's work was not entirely future. In arguably the worst of times, God was still active to advance his plan of redemption. A godly remnant remained faithful in these bleak times, and God worked through them to do more than they could have ever imagined. As we will see, that message applies to us as well.

FOR FURTHER REFLECTION

1. The book of Judges describes a time when Israel experienced what Amos 8:11 calls a famine of hearing the Word of God. Have you lived near or worked with people who have little or no knowledge of the Bible? How were they different from those who do have such knowledge?
2. The West's social commentators and analysts say that we now live in a postmodern age. What distinguishes postmodernism from modernism? How are they, at bottom, similar?
3. If postmodernism resembles the moral chaos in the book of Judges, how might postmodernism be more favorable than modernism for spreading the gospel message? How might it be more challenging for evangelism?
4. Postmodernism abhors and fears absolute authority, yet Christians worship Jesus as the King of kings and Lord of lords. How does Jesus' kingship differ qualitatively from the political and intellectual tyranny that postmodernists, perhaps with good reason, wish to escape?

2

DEVASTATING GRIEF

Given that the book of Ruth is set in the stormy period of the judges, the events of the book occur in the context of spiritual unfaithfulness. As a nation, Israel had sunk into moral debasement and hit rock bottom. We come now to the book of Ruth itself to discover how one family was affected and, more importantly, how God acted to accomplish his purpose through this family during what seemed to be a hopeless era.

Ruth 1:1–5 describes the specific circumstances to which this family, especially the mother-in-law and her daughter-in-law, responded:

> In the days when the judges ruled, there was a famine in the land, and a man from Bethlehem in Judah, together with his wife and two sons, went to live for a while in the country of Moab. The man's name was Elimelech, his wife's name Naomi, and the names of his two sons were Mahlon and Kilion. They were Ephrathites from Bethlehem, Judah. And they went to Moab and lived there.
>
> Now Elimelech, Naomi's husband, died, and she was left with her two sons. They married Moabite women, one named Orpah and the other Ruth. After

they had lived there about ten years, both Mahlon and Kilion also died, and Naomi was left without her two sons and her husband.

As the remainder of Ruth 1 indicates, the same set of circumstances evoked two different responses. This chapter will concentrate on Naomi's. The next chapter will consider Ruth's.

As we look at Ruth 1, I am unaware of my readers' situations and concerns. I do not know what your view of God is or what your expectations of him are in the events of your life. As humans living in a fallen world, none of us is immune to life's hardships and disappointments. We live in a Judges kind of world that tests the sincerity and motives of faith. Ruth 1 addresses God's people who may be feeling battered by life. Perhaps you can identify with Naomi in her suffering and bitterness—even her anger at God.

FROM BAD TO WORSE

Besides the reference to the judges, Ruth 1:1 also says that there was a famine in Israel. Every growing season, people who live in an agrarian economy face the threat of drought, deluge, blight, plague, and the like. When there are no supermarkets, a lean harvest can devastate a community. We know from the book of Judges that people were suffering from violence and anarchy. The opening verse of Ruth informs us that they also had another urgent concern: hunger. With an economy of words, Ruth 1:1 conveys a context of tremendous suffering for all Israel, and there will be more suffering in a particular family before this chapter ends. The barren land that brought on the famine anticipates the barren wombs of Orpah and Ruth as well as Naomi's feelings of barrenness from all the loss that she suffered.[1]

While the more ordinary cause of the famine (and this would not fall outside God's providence) may have been the Midianite incursions of Judges 6:1–6 or even the variable rainfall with which agriculturists must continually contend, the famine may ultimately have been a form of God's judgment against the covenantal unfaithfulness that characterized so much of the judges period. Deuteronomy 28:15–52 lists food shortage as one of the curses for covenantal disobedience. The Jewish Targum (an expansive translation of the Old Testament into Aramaic) understood this famine as one of ten used by God to "reprove the inhabitants of the world."[2]

It may be that the author of Ruth expected us to make a connection between the days of the judges and the deuteronomic curse of food shortage. Even so, the book of Ruth does not explicitly link the famine with punishment. Yet if one comes to Ruth by way of Deuteronomy, Joshua, and Judges, it is hard not to view the famine as both judgment for covenantal disobedience and a wake-up call to repentance. The canonical placement of the book of Ruth, however, has varied throughout the centuries. English translations of the Bible, following the order of the books in the Septuagint or Greek translation of the Old Testament, place Ruth after Judges and before the books of Samuel. The Hebrew Bible, however, has a different location for Ruth. The Hebrew Bible divides the books of the Christian Old Testament into three sections: the Law, Prophets, and Writings. The Law contains the five books of the Pentateuch, and the Prophets include the historical books of Joshua, Judges, Samuel, and Kings along with the three major and the twelve minor prophets. The rest of the books, including Ruth, appear in the Writings. Though Ruth's position within the Writings has been somewhat fluid, the latest scholarly edition of the Hebrew Bible places Ruth between Proverbs and Song of Songs. If this location does not as evidently reflect the influence of Deuteronomy on the book of Ruth, perhaps coming to Ruth by way of Proverbs suggests an association of the woman Ruth with the noble wife of Proverbs 31. Both Ruth and the woman in Proverbs 31 are said to be of noble character. I will suggest later that the writer of Ruth did not want us to focus on the famine as a curse but as an opportunity to practice loving-kindness—a rich Old Testament concept that encompasses compassion, faithfulness, and loyalty.

Unlike previous generations of Old Testament specialists, recent scholarship has tended to invest less effort into isolating the hypothetical stages of the text's composition and more effort into appreciating the literary artistry of the text's final form. Whatever their sources might have been, the biblical writers told engaging stories and crafted poetry with consummate skill. As we shall see, the book of Ruth is no exception. It is a literary masterpiece that humors, intrigues, and exhilarates the reader from start to finish. For example, the opening verses feature several instances of irony.

First, Elimelech and Naomi are said to live in Bethlehem where there was a famine. In Hebrew *Bethlehem* means "house of bread." Ruth 1:1 is saying that the house of bread could not provide for its inhabitants. The irony reminds people of the Judges period and readers of Ruth that the true source of daily bread goes beyond per capita income, the gross national product, or the S&P 500—as seemingly necessary as these might be. Ultimately, God himself provides for our needs (Ps. 136:25; Matt. 6:32), and Paul says that we should do everything, even eating, to God's glory (1 Cor. 10:31). In other words, we should recognize with James 1:17 that every good gift comes from above. During the days of the judges, almost nothing, it seems, was done for God's glory or out of trust in his providence. For this reason, God was not covenantally obligated to send agricultural bounty, and so Israel's breadbasket was empty.

Second, additional irony may be found in Elimelech's name, which means "My God is king." The author of Ruth made no comment about Elimelech's faith, but Elimelech chose to leave the Promised Land. It is possible that the meaning of Elimelech's name never had any significance for him or that life's challenges had progressively eroded his confidence in Israel's divine King. Then again, Elimelech may have been a godly man who, as the patriarchs before him, journeyed outside Canaan not to turn his back on his King but to find food in the short run for his wife and children.[3] He may have gone to Moab in faith that this King would powerfully and graciously watch over him even outside the Promised Land. God had previously done the same for Abraham and Jacob. Or did Elimelech no longer (or not ever) think that Israel's God could care for his needs? Was he now putting his trust in the god of Moab? The text tantalizes but does not answer the questions that it raises.

According to Mira Morgenstern, Elimelech's decision to move to Moab evidenced a selfish concern for his own welfare. One evil (Elimelech's selfishness) then led to another (the marriages of Elimelech's sons to Moabite women), which was compounded by Moab's earlier connection to Sodom through Lot (Gen. 19). Because Sodom "carries multiple connotations of a culture of inhospitality and moral indifference that degenerates into social oppression," Elimelech betrayed his own "moral indifference and acquiescence to sin" by relocating to a place associated with Sodom.[4] Morgenstern may be accurate in her analysis of Elimelech's motive. Nevertheless, whatever the state of Elimelech's relationship with Yahweh, the meaning of his name ironically stood out in the period of the judges when there was no human king in Israel, and just about everyone (Elimelech possibly included) ignored the commands of the divine King.

Third, Elimelech moved his family to Moab. Moab does not have the best reputation in the Old Testament. Deuteronomy 23:3–6 forbade Moabites to worship in God's house or Israelites to befriend them:

> No Ammonite or Moabite or any of his descendants may enter the assembly of the LORD, even down to the tenth generation. For they did not come to meet you with bread and water on your way when you came out of Egypt, and they hired Balaam son of Beor from Pethor in Aram Naharaim to pronounce a curse on you. However, the LORD your God would not listen to Balaam but turned the curse into a blessing for you, because the LORD your God loves you. Do not seek a treaty of friendship with them as long as you live.

History lay behind the prohibition. In Numbers 22, Balak, king of Moab, had hired Balaam to curse the tribes while they were making their way from Egypt to Canaan. Balak, who had heard about Israel's recent defeats of kings Sihon and Og, feared the Israelites and sought any means to gain an advantage over them. To Balak's dismay, his hired diviner, Balaam, uttered favorable oracles for Israel. It seems, though, that Balak's money was well spent for Balaam apparently had a hand in instigating the sordid scene in Numbers 25 (cf. Num. 31:16). Deuteronomy 23:4 summarizes the whole episode by saying that Moab did not offer bread to the Israelites. In other words, it did not show hospitality. Elimelech, then, ironically left the house of bread for Moab that offered no bread. We cannot help but wonder about the wisdom of this decision. Johanna W. H. van Wijk-Bos issues a stronger evaluation: "The very idea of going to Moab for refuge and provisions would be ludicrous."[5]

It is hard to know about Naomi's role in all of this. We do not know if she approved of the move to Moab or of her sons' marriages to Moabite women. Israelites were not supposed to marry Gentiles, and Moab was not the place where good Israelites put down roots or went in search of what they were lacking. Maybe Naomi went with her husband reluctantly. Maybe she was in favor of the move and the marriages. The text does not say. It is silent about why her husband and sons died and why the sons had no children. Could the barrenness of Orpah and Ruth and the deaths of Elimelech, Mahlon, and Kilion have been forms of judgment (Deut. 23:3–6; 28:15–19)? The Jewish Targum thought so, for it considered Mahlon and Kilion's marriages transgressions of the decree of God.[6] Regardless of how we answer these questions that the text raises, Naomi was obviously and understandably devastated on several fronts. She grieved the loss of her husband and children. She had no male protector or provider in a male-dominated world. She was an alien in Moab. Do not miss the desperation of these circumstances with which the book of Ruth confronts its readers at the beginning.

You may be able to relate at some level to these grievous events. You live in an age that is not much different from the time of the judges. First, what is postmodernism but the renunciation of God's truth, God's standards, and God's story? Postmodernism is not really "post-anything." It is Genesis 3 and the book of Judges all over again. Like the characters in the book of Ruth, we live in dark days and troubled times. When people do what is right in their own eyes, some of the oppression that postmodernism appreciably fears from the authoritarianism of modernism results anyways. Second, decisions of other people unavoidably affect you, sometimes adversely. To update the old adage, no one is an island unto himself or herself. We, like Naomi, live with the choices made by a parent, spouse, child, sibling, friend, employer, politician, or criminal. Third, you may feel alone, helpless, anxious, or alienated because of the death of a loved one, the estrangement of a relationship, or the vicissitudes of life. Maybe you feel pounded by pain or, perhaps worse, numbed by pain—either physical or emotional. You may wonder what went wrong or where is God. It is not unusual for God's people to have dark nights of the soul or even dark months and years of the soul. Nowhere does Scripture promise instant relief, much less immunity, from trouble and sorrow. We live in a world that labors under a curse, and the vestiges of the sinful nature still plague us. In Job 5:7, one of Job's friends observes that humans are born to trouble. Here at the beginning of Ruth is trouble times ten.

ONE WOMAN'S RESPONSE TO TRAGEDY

How the text quickly sets the stage in just five verses is instructive. The author did not want us to focus on how Naomi got in this mess. In other words, we should not try to figure out who is most to blame. It is enough for us to know that life in Moab did not turn out as expected. Instead, the author wanted us to pay attention to what happened next. In particular, how did Naomi, Ruth, and Orpah respond to this situation? The clue is not so much their actions as their words. In Hebrew narrative characters are developed more by dialogue than by description.

Naomi's response was to affirm God's sovereignty but not his goodness. While it is true that she prayed Yahweh's kindness (*hesed*) upon Orpah and Ruth, such a prayer may have been more formulaic and polite in contexts of departure (e.g., "Goodbye and Godspeed").[7] Naomi was certainly communicating her inability to help her daughters-in-law. So far as she could tell, there was nothing more that she could do to secure their present or future. Did she think that levirate marriage with Boaz or the nearer kinsman was too far-fetched because Orpah and Ruth were Moabite women? The text does not answer this question. What the text explicitly conveys is that Naomi felt unable to repay the kindness of her daughters-in-law and so bade Yahweh's favor upon them. Danna Nolan Fewell and David M. Gunn suggest that Naomi's polite and seemingly caring words "mask her true intention which is to get rid of Orpah and Ruth," who are "an albatross around her neck."[8] Whatever insight there is to this instance of "reading between the lines," Naomi surely wished them well, for she expressed her hope that Ruth and Orpah would find rest (i.e., provision, protection, and progeny) with another husband. Even so, Naomi was far from convinced that Yahweh is kind. While she acknowledged Ruth and Orpah's kindness to her (Ruth 1:8–9), she said nothing of Yahweh's kindness to her.[9] Several reasons account for her denial of divine goodness.

First, in verse 13 Naomi concluded that her present circumstances betrayed Yahweh's adversarial stance toward her: "It is more bitter for me than for you, because the LORD's hand has gone out against me!" Naomi apparently thought that God had no grievance against Orpah and Ruth per se. Rather, they were being unavoidably and adversely affected by the outpouring of God's disfavor on their mother-in-law. Orpah and Ruth should distance themselves from Naomi lest they continue to experience the disfavor of God because of their association with this spiritual pariah.

Second, in verse 15 Naomi urged Ruth to do as Orpah and return to her gods: "'Look,' said Naomi, 'your sister-in-law is going back to her people and her gods. Go back with her.'" This piece of maternal advice does not fit well with the earlier blessing in Yahweh's name. Naomi may have thought that Orpah and Ruth's nationality excluded them from Yahweh's interest. They would conceivably fare better under the care of the Moabite deity, Chemosh. Such reasoning on Naomi's part may seem strange, but people in the ancient Near East tended to have a localized view of a god's efficacy in the lives of his or her devotees. Although the Israelites confessed the universality of Yahweh's reach and the exclusivity of his influence, Naomi's theology had apparently become eclectic in Moab. Perhaps, because of the theologically aberrant climate of the judges period, Naomi's theology never was too well formulated or constrained by revelation.

Third, in verses 20–21 Naomi used two names for God to draw certain conclusions about his providential activity in her life:

> "Don't call me Naomi," she told them. "Call me Mara, because the Almighty has made my life very bitter. I went away full, but the LORD has brought me back empty. Why call me Naomi? The Lord has afflicted [or witnessed against] me; the Almighty has brought misfortune upon me."

Using the more general name Almighty (Shaddai), which emphasizes the superior power of God over humans, Naomi claimed that God had made her life bitter and, to translate literally, had done evil to her. Naomi believed that God as Almighty exercised unrivaled control over her life. To her way of thinking, however, that control was not necessarily tempered by an inclination toward kindness. Using the covenantal name LORD (Yahweh), which emphasizes the responsibility of relationship, Naomi alleged that God had brought her back to Bethlehem empty and had witnessed against her—a possible association of Naomi's misfortune with the curses of Deuteronomy 28. Naomi apparently believed that God as Yahweh had administered retribution for her family's unfaithfulness to the covenantal stipulations.[10] Or possibly she shared the viewpoint of Job's friends and many moderns that suffering is, more generally and less covenantally, the consequence of wrongdoing.

It is evident that Naomi's circumstances influenced her to develop a hardened understanding of divine sovereignty. Reg Grant observes: "[Naomi] looked at her situation and said in effect, 'This bitterness is the only reality I know or that can be known. This is "truth," and by it I will redefine my concept of God.'"[11] For Naomi, her circumstances indicated that God is great but not good. He may be able to do with her as he pleases (and who can argue?), but his pleasure lacks empathy and kindness. With such distorted (i.e., circumstance-dependent) theology and a crushed spirit, she never prayed. Instead, she despaired, resigning herself to the inevitable machinations of a cruel deity.

The text, however, has not told us that God was angry with Naomi. She was therefore mistaken to measure God's goodness by her level of happiness or her immediate circumstances. What is more, she appeared to remember the past too selectively and/or nostalgically. While the title of this book is *From Famine to Fullness*, Naomi would have, at this point, entitled her autobiography *From Fullness to Famine*. She seemed to have forgotten that conditions in Bethlehem ten years ago (or more) had driven Elimelech to abandon his homeland. While it is true that Naomi had lost a husband and two sons, saying that she left Bethlehem full ignores the reason why she left at all. Life had treated her harshly in Bethlehem, just as it more recently had battered her in Moab.

We often do this, do we not? We judge God's love and faithfulness by how many of our desires have been met.[12] When our desires do not materialize, our words are telling. Angry, accusing words reveal the idols of our hearts—so do selfish prayers couched in pious and deferential language. Too often, it is not God's will that we want, but our will made possible by God. Had not Naomi made God the servant of her agenda? Do we not do the same?

To be sure, Naomi's grief and predicament were real, and we cannot read Ruth 1 without having our hearts go out to this woman. The compressed account gives the impression that her world had come crashing down rather suddenly. Even if as many as ten years separated her sons' deaths from her husband's death, Naomi had experienced an inordinate amount of death, disappointment, and grief in that time. Moreover, her losses were never relieved by the births of grandchildren. Given the pathos of her situation, can we make concessions about her words in Ruth 1? Were her grief and predicament so devastating that Naomi distraughtly and almost unconsciously uttered statements that she did not mean and would not otherwise have said in less challenging circumstances? This approach, however pastorally sensitive its motive might be, seems unlikely because Hebrew narrative typically develops characters through dialogue. The reader discovers what is in the heart of the character by what he or she reportedly says.

Even if the author of Ruth preserved words that are more emotionally charged than rationally measured, Naomi cannot be excused from sinning with her tongue. God's people should exercise self-control in any circumstance and seek to honor him at all times and in all places. If self-control is part of the fruit of the Spirit, the Bible does not put limits on it so that God's people may blaspheme during the grimmest and most shattering moments. Instead, the Bible teaches that "no temptation has seized you except what is common to man" (1 Cor. 10:13). This observation, however, does not proceed from a Stoic philosopher who had a take-life-as-it-comes, grin-and-bear-it, or keep-a-stiff-upper-lip outlook. It comes from Paul, who could list his own dreadful instances of suffering (2 Cor. 11:23–28). Paul's ministry and letters reveal a Christian who would not let go of a God who foreordains whatever comes to pass—for the glory of his Son and the good of his people. Paul believed that God would not test his people beyond what they could bear and maintained in the midst of an unidentified source of personal affliction that perseverance in godliness was possible:

> To keep me from becoming conceited because of these surpassingly great revelations, there was given me a thorn in my flesh, a messenger of Satan, to

torment me. Three times I pleaded with the Lord to take it away from me. But he said to me, "My grace is sufficient for you, for my power is made perfect in weakness." Therefore I will boast all the more gladly about my weaknesses, so that Christ's power may rest on me. That is why, for Christ's sake, I delight in weaknesses, in insults, in hardships, in persecutions, in difficulties. For when I am weak, then I am strong. (2 Cor. 12:7–10)

Here was no armchair theologian, but a faithful servant who theologized in the rigors of the temptations that beset every believer. His words indicated that his theology controlled his response to the challenging vicissitudes of life.

Similarly, Job comes to mind. No one would minimize his loss, even when compared to Naomi's.[13] His servants died in a raid by the Chaldeans who stole his property. His children died from what we would call a natural disaster. His health failed to the point that he suffered unrelieved pain. The biblical writer observed, first, that "Job did not sin by charging God with wrongdoing" (Job 1:22) and, second, that he "did not sin in what he said" (Job 2:10). That Job later repented for demanding to speak with God as an equal does not detract from the tenacity of his faith in a time of unparalleled loss, grief, and confusion. He never followed his wife's advice to curse God and die. Rather, his speech continually manifested an unshakable commitment to the God who sovereignly governed his circumstances— both favorable and unfavorable.

In Ruth 1 Naomi was struggling to transcend her circumstances and trust God in them. In the face of so much calamity, Naomi made seemingly logical decisions. What is more, she imposed her logic on Orpah and Ruth. Yet her logic betrayed self-absorption that was blind to what God was doing. She was ruled by her circumstances instead of the Lord of her circumstances. Consequently, she did not view her situation as an opportunity to minister. How could a daughter of Abraham with a clear conscience have instructed her Moabite daughters-in-law to return to their gods? André LaCocque tries to soften the bluntness of Naomi's reasoning by claiming that "Naomi recommends a return not to the deities of Moab, but to a socially established security."[14] To be sure, social security had been a part of Naomi's counsel all along, but Naomi disturbingly linked security with idolatry. By sending Orpah and Ruth back to their gods, Naomi broke the first commandment and denied its practical application to a specific case. Because the one true God was allegedly not sufficient to grant security to all who trust in him, regardless of national and social background, Orpah and Ruth had to resort to other gods. Naomi further denied the Abrahamic covenant, which views the Israelites as the channel of redemptive blessing to everyone else. Naomi responded naturally and logically with a human-centered strategy. Her response was not informed by Israel's theology, which had its source in the self-revealing God of the patriarchs, Moses, and Joshua. How often to this point in God's relationship with his people had he performed a mighty deed that turned around an ostensibly hopeless situation? Naomi forgot her theology, or maybe she, living in the days of the judges, never knew it.

Now the question is whether you view the situations of your life as part of God's plan. This text challenges you to believe that God is active in your life even when it hurts. In fact, the whole book teaches about God's providence in our lives. He is not only in control but also up to something good, namely, the accomplishment of his redemptive plan and the perfection of his people. The challenge of walking by faith is to see the situations of your life as opportunities to glorify Jesus Christ. Too often, though, we think that the situations of our lives are about what we want. What is your view of God, then, when your desires are not met? Do you still consider him faithful and caring, or has he failed to render obligatory services?

God does not enter into relationship with us to give everything that we think we want. He draws us to himself that we might find security, contentment, peace, and joy in him. To get us to that point, he sometimes uses difficult times to show us our dependence. He may use the consequences of our sin or of somebody else's sin. He may use hardship that is traceable to nobody's sin. He brings us to a point of weakness to demonstrate his greatness and goodness. Weaned from carnal affections, we delight in what is dear to God's heart, entrust ourselves to his care, and let him work in our circumstances for his glory.

Naomi had not learned to do that yet, at least not completely. Neither have we. Entrusting ourselves to God and seeing what he does take a lifetime. In that lifetime God makes changes in us that prepare us for an eternity with him. Eternity puts our present circumstances into proper perspective. Paul, in the context of describing his troubles in 2 Corinthians 4:17, went so far as to use the words "light" and "momentary": "For our light and momentary troubles are achieving for us and eternal glory that far outweighs them all." He was on board with what God was up to in his life. God has not chosen to mature his people immediately, and he does not reconcile all things to his eternal plan in the blink of an eye. Still, whatever trials and joys come our way serve his good purpose for our lives and ultimately his kingdom. Though Paul, like us, could not fully know what God was up to in the events of his life, he was willing to be faithful in whatever challenges confronted him day by day. Paul looked beyond the present difficulty and anticipated the good that God would accomplish— what he calls eternal glory.

THE PRESENCE OF
GOD'S GRACE AND PURPOSE

How do we know this, though? Notice that God showed grace in the wayward and painful times of the judges. Ruth 1:6 and 1:22 speak of a reversal of fortune brought about by Yahweh. In 1:6 Naomi learned that Yahweh "had come to the aid of his people by providing food for them." The Hebrew word translated "had come to the aid" has the root meaning of "to visit" and occurs numerous times throughout the Old Testament, often with reference to Israel's observance of the covenant. Because Yahweh visits to bless or punish his people, context determines whether God's visits are favorable or not. Here in Ruth 1, Yahweh's provision of food (literally bread) during a famine in the days of the judges clearly introduced grace into the story that ensued. God had not abandoned his people to their just deserts or to random fate. Instead, he was graciously acting in history to preserve them. Verse 22 confirms the good news with a reference to the barley harvest as Naomi returned to Bethlehem. God had indeed blessed the growing season so that Bethlehem would live up to its name. The famine had ended, and a bounteous harvest would fill the granaries.

Even so, we cannot appreciate verses 6 and 22 unless we affirm God's justice, and God's justice means condemnation for covenant-breakers. God is not obligated to pity and pardon those who break his commands. Ruth 1:6 attests not to the goodness and worthiness of humanity but to the grace of God. However we might evaluate Elimelech and Naomi, Ruth 1:1 has set Yahweh's provision of food in the context of the apostasy of the judges period. Why does God choose to be gracious to sinners when he does not have to be? What is going on here in Ruth 1:6 is part of the movement of redemptive history. God is active in history to redeem a people for his name, and redemption gets at God's ultimate reason for paying attention to humans. Through our redemption God exalts his Son, who is the Redeemer. Romans 8:29 says, "For those God foreknew he also predestined to be conformed to the likeness of his Son, that he might be the firstborn among many brothers." The word "firstborn" has to do with rank or position. God loves his people to be sure, and Romans 8:39 states that nothing can separate God's people from his love. Even so, God's love is a means to an end. The plan of salvation ultimately is not about us but about the preeminence of Jesus who saves us. By means of our salvation that has been accomplished by Jesus' humiliating death, God in his infinite wisdom has exalted his Son over all creation.

This exaltation of God's Son enables Christians to read Ruth 1:21 without fear. Naomi thought that Yahweh was, in effect, testifying against her in a court of law. He had allegedly turned against her. According to Romans 8:33, no one, not even God himself, will bring charges against God's elect sons and daughters. Jesus Christ intercedes on behalf of those who are united to him by faith. Christians may experience the effects of living in a fallen world; they may undergo the refining discipline of a loving Father; but nothing can reverse the justification that God has declared on the strength of Christ's active obedience (his perfect keeping of the law, called righteousness, that is imputed to believers) and his passive obedience (his suffering and death that represent the imputation of believers' sins and their punishment for sin to him). If God has promised to exalt his Son through the accomplishment of the plan of redemption, then we can be sure that he will care for us. God keeps his word because his reputation is at stake.

God does not abandon us to our sin or the effects of other people's choices. He has acted in Jesus Christ to save you from your sin and to redeem his creation. To be sure, Naomi's situation looked bleak, but God's finest moment in her life was about to begin. Likewise, God is at work in the situations of our life to accomplish his good plan. That plan is to exalt Jesus Christ in his people. What God has already done in Jesus Christ is proof. He has not brought us this far in Christ to renege on his plan and promise. We can be patient, temperate, and hopeful in times of stress and distress.

FOR FURTHER REFLECTION

1. Does Naomi's situation in Ruth 1 remind you of a time or times in your life when loss and grief overwhelmed you? Describe how your perspective of God is affected by emotional and physical pain. What other circumstances alter your view of God?

2. Naomi is not the only person who has spoken so honestly about her experience of a frowning providence. The psalmist regularly did. Have you ever been angry at God and accused him of wanting to make your life miserable? Describe the occasion.

3. Naomi's advice to Ruth to go back to her gods may sound shocking on the lips of an Israelite. To what gods are you tempted to return when life is turned upside down and the God and Father of our Lord Jesus Christ seems to be remote?

4. How is it possible for you to confess God's love for his people, even for you, when circumstances would suggest otherwise? Stated differently, what is the Christian's assurance of salvation?

5. How might a suffering, confused, and even angry Christian pray during a dark night of the soul?

6. How can God's ultimate purpose to exalt his Son over all creation give you comfort and perspective in the changing times of your life?

3

BEYOND WHAT
WOULD BE EXPECTED

I f the previous chapter considered Naomi's reaction to the devastating events described in Ruth 1:1–5, this chapter examines Ruth's response to those same circumstances. In particular, we will seek to understand and appreciate Ruth's justly famous affirmation of loyalty in Ruth 1:16–17:

> But Ruth replied, "Don't urge me to leave you or to turn back from you. Where you go I will go, and where you stay I will stay. Your people will be my people and your God my God. Where you die I will die, and there I will be buried. May the LORD deal with me, be it ever so severely, if anything but death separates you and me."

We recognize these words because they are occasionally used in wedding ceremonies. Ruth and brides may have in common the joining of new families, but the similarity stops there. Ruth's pledge had nothing to do with marriage. Even though marriage to Boaz would come later, neither Ruth nor Naomi had any way of knowing about that now. Rather, Ruth pledged her loyalty to her mother-in-law. An earlier marriage had brought them together, and the vicissitudes of life now gave them even more common ground. They both had lost the same men (Elimelech, Mahlon, and Kilion) whom they had loved for different, but related, reasons.

WHY RUTH STAYED WITH NAOMI

Ruth's stated reason for staying with Naomi went beyond familial ties. Ruth had come to know the covenant God of Israel. Her commitment to Yahweh lay behind her commitment to Naomi, and what commitment she showed! In Ruth we see how true saving faith led to conduct that was beyond what would have been expected. The same should be true for us.

Perhaps Naomi's loss was more grievous—a husband and two sons. She was also older and less likely to remarry. But Ruth's situation was by no means less serious. Perhaps she could return to her Moabite family, but we do not know if they would have accepted her. She had, after all, married a foreign man, even an Israelite. Moabites were hardly sympathetic with the Israelites' conquest of Canaan. They had indirectly lost land to Israel when Israel conquered the Amorite king, Sihon, who had previously dispossessed the Moabites of some of their territory (Num. 21:26). Numbers 22–25 also records the association of the Moabites with the Midianites in the sordid events of the Balaam debacle. That the Moabites knew of the exclusive claims of Israel's religion should not be overlooked either. While it is unknown how religious Elimelech, Naomi, Mahlon, and Kilion were, even a nominal commitment of her in-laws to Yahweh could have ostracized Ruth from her family and friends. Such reaction has happened throughout history when a son or daughter has married outside the family's religion, ethnicity, or race. Ruth's future, then, was just as uncertain as Naomi's. Ruth committed herself to a disillusioned older woman who apparently had nothing. Moreover, Ruth left her homeland for a land where she would hardly have been welcome. Time would tell just how difficult it would be for Ruth to be accepted. Sometimes the longer a person stays in a new place, the more he or she realizes that he or she will never fit.

In some sense, though, Ruth announced her intention to change her identity. Adele Berlin explains how "almost inconceivable" this would be in Ruth's context:

> The ancient world had no mechanism for religious conversion or change of citizenship; the very notion was unthinkable. Religion and peoplehood defined one's ethnic identity, and this could no more be changed than the color of one's skin. A Moabite was always a Moabite, wherever he or she lived. And, indeed, Ruth is referred to throughout the story as "the Moabitess." But from Ruth's point of view, she is becoming an Israelite. She is joining herself to Naomi not only on the private family level, but also on the national peoplehood level.[1]

It is uncertain how nationally conscious the Israelites were during the days of the judges and if Ruth thought that she was changing her nationality. Regarding the constitution of early Israel, John Bright noted that "Israel . . . was made up of elements of heterogeneous origin [Ex. 12:38], and she was held together by no central government or machinery of state." Bright went on to say that the tribes and those outsiders who joined themselves to the tribes were held together by a covenant rooted in the mighty deeds of Yahweh. This "new society" was "based not in blood, but in historical experience and moral decision."[2] When the tribes, as seen in the book of Judges, forgot their history and strayed from the covenant, they began to lose their distinctiveness and melded with the Canaanites who remained in the land. Still, the book of Ruth indicates that a godly remnant remained in Canaan, and it is to this group that Ruth, out of theological conviction and familial loyalty, joined herself, as unlikely as that decision may have seemed to Naomi, Orpah, or anyone else at the time.

What Ruth seems to have known was that the God of Israel accepted people regardless of background. How Ruth knew this about Yahweh is hard to say. Ruth 1 does not give the impression that Naomi was an energetic evangelist. According to James C. Howell, "Naomi is hardly the kind of winsome witness sometimes paraded in church life today."[3] Still, Ruth's faith apparently owed something to her in-laws. Ruth had learned about God's covenant and put her trust in God's promises. At the very least, Ruth, like Rahab (Josh. 2:10), must have heard the reports of Israel's escape from Egypt and defeat of Sihon and Og. If Ruth attributed these stunning events to Yahweh, then she, too, could have come to faith in the God of Israel upon hearing of his mighty deeds.

The text is clear about why Ruth stuck with Naomi. While it cannot be denied that Ruth cared for her mother-in-law, Ruth clung to Naomi because of her devotion to the God of Naomi's people. The Hebrew word translated "clung" in Ruth 1:14 is used of the Israelites' relation to Yahweh. They were commanded by Moses to hold fast to Yahweh:

> Fear the LORD your God and serve him. Hold fast to him and take your oaths in his name. (Deut. 10:20)

> It is the LORD your God you must follow, and him you must revere. Keep his commands and obey him; serve him and hold fast to him. (Deut. 13:4)

Joshua repeated the same command in Joshua 23:8: "But you are to hold fast to the LORD your God, as you have until now." In Ruth 1:16, Ruth exhibited the essence of clinging by her modification of the covenant motto. Instead of "I will be your God and you will be my people," Ruth affirmed that God and God's people would be hers. She had renounced her Moabite identity and entrusted her destiny to Naomi's God.

The Aramaic Targum captures the sense of verse 16 with the following expansion: "Ruth said, 'Do not urge me to leave you, to go back from after you for I desire to be a proselyte.'"[4] What God had done through the descendants of Abraham had accomplished its intended purpose of drawing this Gentile to faith. "Proselyte," though, may be too weak a term. Ruth underwent more than a religious conversion. Perhaps more accurately stated, Ruth's religious conversion included a willingness to forsake all other ties—familial, ethnic, and national. Did she understand even more than many of the Israelites what it meant to be a daughter of Abraham and part of the people of God? Blood descent from Abraham did not assure one of relationship with Abraham's God (John 8:31–47; Rom. 2:28–29; 9:6–8). Rather, one had Abraham as his or her spiritual father if he or she shared Abraham's faith in Yahweh and observed Yahweh's commands.[5]

Ruth's background may, in fact, have provided an advantage for understanding the benefits of being in covenant with Yahweh. According to Bonnie Honig,

> . . . it is Ruth's *foreignness* that enables her to choose the Israelites in a meaningful way. Indeed, the more radical her foreignness, the more meaningful the sense of chosenness that results from her choosing. The more deep the enmity between Moab and Israel, the more profound the friendship that is declared in its midst. The more radically particular the convert,

the more obviously universal the divinity that compels her to join up.[6]

In other words, Ruth as an outsider did not take for granted the benefits of being in covenant with Yahweh. She had experienced the alternative of not being in covenant with him. Honig further suggests that the conversion of someone so different, like Ruth, would renew the appreciation of the Israelites for the compelling truth about Yahweh.[7] Ruth's godliness obviously impressed Boaz. How much it may have awakened other Bethlehemites out of spiritual torpor is unknown.

Ruth's devotion to this God who saves irrespective of nationality led her to make unusual decisions. Rather than take the seemingly safer option of staying in Moab, Ruth threw herself on the mercy and care of the God of Israel. Her trust in a covenant-making God led her to abandon all other sources of security. Laura E. Donaldson reports how Cherokee women, for example, identify with Orpah who "connotes hope rather than perversity, because she is the one who does not reject her traditions or her sacred ancestors."[8] If Orpah followed the sensible advice of Naomi, Ruth, it would seem, threw caution to the wind and made a foolish decision. She cast her lot with a destitute mother-in-law in an alien land.

This mother-in-law, in spite of her grief, certainly possessed an undiminished capacity to assess a predicament. Naomi's reasoning in Ruth 1:12–13 was incontrovertible:

> Return home, my daughters; I am too old to have another husband. Even if I thought there was still hope for me—even if I had a husband tonight and then gave birth to sons—would you wait until they grew up? Would you remain unmarried for them?

Even if it was still biologically possible for Naomi to give birth to a third son, Ruth would perhaps be beyond childbearing years when that son was old enough to marry and father children. What is seemingly worse, though unstated, is that the residents of Naomi's homeland were in covenant with a God who disallowed his people to befriend Ruth's people. Why would Naomi or her potential son want to become entangled with the social and religious implications of a(nother) mixed marriage? The stigma would bring only further grief. By the time the son reached manhood, the years would have moved along, and everyone by then would want to bury the past—everyone, it seems, but Ruth.

FAITH IN THE MIGHTY ACTS OF GOD

What is to be learned from Ruth's loyalty to Naomi and to Yahweh? In Ruth we see that true saving faith is not exercised in a purely abstract or academic setting. Faith cannot be reduced to the result of analytic and dispassionate reasoning about the question of God that characteristically arises in the philosophy of religion. Faith must be lived out in the vicissitudes of normal life.

To be sure, faith involves the intellect and so is neither blind nor irrational. There was and is intellectual content to the worship and service of Yahweh, who is a self-revealing God. For this reason, the Bible contains as much historical narrative as it does. These records show God in action to disclose his identity and accomplish his purpose. Time and again, God announced what he would do, did it, and then interpreted what had happened. These events and their interpretation comprise the content of biblical faith. If the Athenians later had an altar to an unknown God (Acts 17:23), the Israelites had no excuse for being ignorant of the God of their fathers and no warrant for conceiving of God according to human categories of thought. Yahweh was and is both transcendent and personal. While he cannot be limited by the constraints of human reason, he has freely entered humanity's frame of reference to make himself known.

From Ruth's vantage point, Yahweh had said that he would deliver his people from oppression in Egypt and give them an inheritance in Canaan. Whatever can be said about the time of the judges and the relocation of at least one Israelite family outside the Promised Land, God had delivered Canaan into the possession of his people. They, as the fewest of all peoples (Deut. 7:7), had stupendously broken the back of the Canaanites and inhabited their cities. Ruth must have been aware of these historical developments and their theological interpretation.

Not to be overlooked, of course, were the numerous times that God acted in ostensibly hopeless situations. It is hard to hear the stories of the patriarchs, exodus, and conquest and miss the truth of Gabriel's words to Mary in Luke 1:37. When Mary heard the angelic annunciation of her pregnancy, she protested that she was a virgin. Gabriel then asserted, "For nothing is impossible with God." Who would have thought that Sarah could have given birth to Isaac, Rebekah to twins, or Rachel to Joseph and later Benjamin? Who would have imagined Jacob's return to Canaan and reconciliation with Esau after years of exile in Paddan Aram? Could anyone have foreseen unlikable Judah's impassioned speeches before Jacob and Joseph by which he, at potentially great cost to himself and with uncharacteristic concern for his father, guaranteed Benjamin's safety and then pled for his release? How unlikely Joseph's reconciliation with his brothers after so long a separation or Moses' return to Egypt to liberate the Israelites after fleeing from justice and herding sheep for decades. Is there a strictly naturalistic explanation for the crossing of the Red Sea or the provision of food and water in the wilderness or the defeat of the Canaanites? Being married to an Israelite man, Ruth surely had heard these accounts of the extended family history and could appreciate the unlikelihood of any of these developments.

Even so, faith goes beyond knowledge of core data and assents to the veracity of the data. One can read or hear a report and choose not to believe it. In Ruth's case, she could not deny that the Israelites lived in Canaan after escaping from Egypt and defeating a number of kings along the way. Although she could have given a different explanation to the data, such as every once in a while the underdog beats the odds, Ruth evidently accepted the Israelites' report of their God's show of strength on their behalf. If Israel was the least of all peoples, her string of victories strained believability, unless a strong Advocate was on her side. This is what Israel officially claimed, and Ruth must have assented to the claim despite the contrary evidence of the judges period.

Ruth then allowed the implications of the data to effect personal change. She forsook her Moabite identity and associated with the covenant community of Israel. Knowledge and assent led to active trust. Ruth put her faith into action and made concrete changes in her life. She turned from a former way of life to a new identity among Yahweh's people. Others could see these fruits of trust and note that a change of direction had occurred. Boaz said as much during their first meeting:

> Boaz replied, "I've been told all about what you have done for your mother-in-law since the death of your husband—how you left your father and mother and your homeland and came to live with a people you did not know before. May the LORD repay you for what you have done. May you be richly rewarded by the LORD, the God of Israel, under whose wings you have come to take refuge." (Ruth 2:11–12)

This change of direction occurred, however, in the context of personal upheaval and emotional distress. When

Ruth declared that her mother-in-law's God would be her God, there was nothing calm and ideal about her circumstances. Along with Naomi, Ruth had suffered a devastating loss that made her future insecure. Nevertheless, she, a Moabitess, affirmed the essence of the Abrahamic covenant. Indeed, her faith surpassed Abraham's because she had no personal command or promise from Yahweh. Rather, she acted on what God had promised to Abraham—in devastating and dire circumstances no less. She surely knew the risks from a human perspective, but the God of Israel (her God by faith) was, to her way of thinking, bigger than the situation. It is evident from the rest of the book and her inclusion in Jesus' genealogy in Matthew 1 that God credited her faith to her as righteousness, just as he had credited Abraham's faith.

By contrast, Orpah apparently permitted the risks to outweigh any confidence that she might have had in Naomi's God. However sincere, Naomi had prayed that Orpah and Ruth would find other husbands. The book never says if Naomi's prayer was answered in Orpah's case. She was forgotten. The rest of the book of Ruth will explain how Naomi's prayer was answered in the case of the woman who boldly put her faith in Yahweh and committed her future to him.

So then, faith involves a commitment of the will to trust the self-revealing God of the Bible in the uncertainties and vicissitudes of everyday life. Faith in the God of the Bible, however, is not a leap in the dark. Just as Ruth surely knew the history of God's relationship with Israel, New Testament believers similarly know that same history and how it climaxes in Jesus Christ. God has done mighty deeds to secure our redemption. Think of Jesus' miracles that represent reversals of the effects of the curse for sin, or the raising of Jesus from the dead as proof of God's satisfaction with his sacrifice for our sins, or the ascension by which Jesus was exalted as God's vice-regent over all creation or the present intercessory ministry of Jesus as high priest. Not to be overlooked as well is our own history as individuals and as groups of believers. We can look back and see God's faithfulness to us and to his church.

In all these deeds God has displayed his greatness and goodness. He is great and powerful to take care of us in all situations. He is good and gracious to want to take care of us. The proof is what he has already done for us through Jesus Christ. In Christ God has expiated our sins and propitiated his wrath. He, the heavenly judge, has adopted us sinners into his family and promised to care for us. He has given us his Spirit that we might be conformed to Christ's likeness. If God has done all this, what are the situations of our lives but opportunities for God to advance his good purpose? God has demonstrated his commitment to his people, and the situations of our lives are now the stage on which God continues to prove his love and faithfulness—for our maturation in godliness as well as for a witness to those who observe what God is doing through us. So then, we need not be afraid or despairing. God is neither dead nor distant. He is on site in our lives, as complex as they may be, to accomplish his will, which, among other things, is to teach us that he is all-sufficient for our every need and worry.

HOW FAITH ACTS

How then should God's people live where God has put them? People who put their faith in Yahweh respond to their circumstances not with self-centered strategies for coping but with obedience and trust that sometimes defy conventional thinking. If God is active in history, daring to entrust one's well-being and future into his care becomes the sensible course to take. To try to direct our own lives according to conventional, worldly wisdom will always come up short in the face of so many unforeseen and unmanageable variables. We are neither omniscient nor omnipotent and so unable to take control of our lives. Ruth seemed to understand this reality. Sixteen verses into the book, she modeled a mature faith and abandoned her security, her reputation, and her future not just to a nebulous higher power called God (Elohim) but to the self-revealing LORD (Yahweh), the covenant-making and covenant-keeping God of the past, present, and future. She did not have to worry about marital status (hers or Naomi's), sons, place of residence, sustenance, or even death. She swore by Yahweh in Ruth 1:17 because she, as Boaz would later note (2:12), had taken her refuge in him. Long before Paul wrote it, Ruth knew the truth of Romans 8:28, that "in all things God works for the good of those who love him." She could deduce the assurance of God's sustaining grace from the revelation and experience of his redeeming grace. What she knew to be true of God trumped any momentary circumstance.

Your need may differ from that for which Naomi prayed on behalf of Ruth, but the same God hears your prayers. Those who commit themselves to the covenant God of the Bible and trust him to care for them discover that he is attentive to their needs and longings. God's Word affirms over and over that he does not turn a deaf ear to the petitions of those who approach him contritely yet confidently. He who knows the details of our lives intimately delights to weave those details into a tapestry that, upon completion, manifests the consummate skill of the One who arranges all threads into a meaningful and glorious whole.

Jesus calls us to seek first the kingdom of God (Matt. 6:33). That means, in part, seeing our circumstances as divine appointments to serve Jesus Christ. This is no less an act of faith than Ruth's decision to leave Moab for Israel. Rarely do we know how our service will turn out.

Certainly Ruth did not. In fact, her faith initially met with Naomi's indifference.

At the end of Ruth 1, Naomi returned to Bethlehem and met acquaintances and friends from long ago. While they made a fuss over her, Naomi told them that Yahweh had actively desired to inflict deprivation and misery on her. So convinced was she that she could not stand for them to call her by her birth name, Naomi, which means "pleasant" or "sweet." Instead, she distanced herself from memories of happier days in the past and changed her name to Mara, which means "bitter." Ten years after leaving Bethlehem because of a famine, she complained that God had brought her back empty. In other words, the famine had occurred in stages that left Naomi feeling increasingly desolate and deprived: first a shortage of food, then a loss of family, and now internal emptiness.[9] To be sure, Naomi did not return with her husband, sons, and Orpah, but she also did not return empty or alone. Ruth was with her and devoted to her. Naomi, however, did not seem too eager to introduce Ruth to the people of Bethlehem and, in fact, brushed her off indirectly with references to emptiness and misfortune. Perhaps Naomi was embarrassed in front of the homefolks by a Moabite daughter-in-law.

Naomi might not have been able or willing at this time to see God's blessing in her daughter-in-law, but Ruth embodied Yahweh's presence with Naomi for good, not ill. Later, these same women of Bethlehem would acknowledge as much when they praised Yahweh for a kinsman-redeemer and then stunningly extolled Ruth as being better than seven sons (Ruth 4:15). The point is that God had never abandoned Naomi or turned against her. Ruth was the assurance of God's love, care, and purpose all along the way.

While it is tempting to focus on Ruth's magnanimity in the face of Naomi's slight, we would do better to dwell on Ruth's steadfast love. Her commitment to Naomi was eventually used of God to restore Naomi's fortunes. Presumably also, the hints of Naomi's brightening countenance in Ruth 2 and 3 should also lead us to recognize the restoration of Naomi's faith. Though Naomi does not speak in Ruth 4, she also does not curse God after Ruth 1. Naomi, of course, would wish for the return of her husband and sons. Even so, Ruth's loyalty helped Naomi see the goodness of God again and possibly reach the point, with the benefit of hindsight, of being able to thank God for the dark days—or at least recognize the wisdom of God in them.

The same is true for God's people today. Experiencing the grace of God in Jesus Christ should lead as it did with Ruth to charitable conduct toward others. God's goodness and our charity are related as root and fruit. Deuteronomy repeatedly instructed the Israelites to respond to the plight of the disadvantaged and alien in the same kind, caring, and advocating way that God had treated them when they were oppressed strangers in Egypt:

> Remember that you were slaves in Egypt and the LORD your God redeemed you. That is why I give you this command today. (Deut. 15:15; cf. Deut. 24:18)

> Remember that you were slaves in Egypt, and follow carefully these decrees. (Deut. 16:12)

Similarly, those whom God has richly blessed in Jesus Christ are to treat others graciously and generously:

> Share with God's people who are in need. Practice hospitality. (Rom. 12:13)

> For you know the grace of our Lord Jesus Christ, that though he was rich, yet for your sakes he became

poor, so that you through his poverty might become rich. . . . Each man should give what he has decided in his heart to give, not reluctantly or under compulsion, for God loves a cheerful giver. And God is able to make all grace abound to you, so that in all things at all times, having all that you need, you will abound in every good work. (2 Cor. 8:9; 9:7–8)

Command them to do good, to be rich in good deeds, and to be generous and willing to share. (1 Tim. 6:18)

When God's people act this way toward others, God often uses such kindness as the means for introducing redemptive hope where it is needed.

What is so jolting in Ruth 1 is that the one soon to be an alien (Ruth the Moabitess) came to the support of the one soon to be the resident (Naomi the Israelitess). Perhaps Ruth was accustomed to being an advocate for her foreign mother-in-law while they lived in Moab. Now her newly declared faith in the God of Naomi became the basis for her loyalty and support. Ruth put her faith to work immediately, and God blessed others through her.

The New Testament likens Christians to a body (1 Cor. 12:12–31). Each member of the body has been blessed by God with abilities and resources that can serve others. Even when a believer is faltering in his or her faith, a brother or sister in the Lord should come alongside and build up the one who is weak. Ruth held up Naomi. Whom has God brought into your life to encourage and enrich? How can your commitment to Jesus Christ be manifested in conduct toward others that goes beyond what is expected? As in the case of Ruth with Naomi, the results of such investment in the life of another may not be immediately seen, but going beyond the conventional or the expected provides the stage on which God often does the unexpected.

FOR FURTHER REFLECTION

1. Have you ever had to assimilate into another culture or subculture? What do you think was on Ruth's mind as she made the choice to leave her culture and go to another that she knew only through her in-laws?

2. What uncertainties come with pledging your loyalty to another person? Is pledging your loyalty to God different from committing yourself to a human?

3. Have you ever "gone out on a limb" for another person, even someone who may not have been a likely candidate for such steadfastness? Why did you do it? Did you receive confirmation that God had used you to advance his purpose in that person's life?

4. What does it mean for you to join the family of God?

5. In your experience, what aspects of the Christian life seem illogical at first glance but then make sense within the biblical worldview?

4

HOLY RISKS

We all know that the Bible calls us to trust God, but what does trust look like? Do we trust God only at extraordinary moments, or does God also call us to trust him in the seemingly mundane events of our lives? Ruth 2 helps us understand what it means to trust God.

Before considering the look of trust, we have to establish the foundation of trust. For what reason would we put our trust in God? We might blindly put our trust in God and have a rather shaky conviction about the reliability of the object of our trust. We might hope that God will come through for us but not have any way to be sure. Or maybe trust in God is more than a shot in the dark, and there is a firm basis for putting our confidence in him. Ruth 2:3 creatively explains the foundation for the believer's trust. Let me set the stage.

THE OLD TESTAMENT'S SAFETY NET

Naomi and Ruth returned to Bethlehem because they had heard that there was food again. The availability of food, however, did not automatically alleviate hunger. Somebody had to "bring home the bacon." If we recall that *Bethlehem* means "house of bread," then Greg A. King has aptly noted, "This 'house of bread' was no cornucopia for them"—at least not immediately.[1] Whatever the status of Elimelech's property (to be discussed in a later chapter), Naomi and Ruth did not have a crop to harvest or money to buy food from someone else. Moreover, Naomi gave no indication that the nearer kinsman, Boaz, or anyone else was available to help. The immediate situation for these two widows was nothing short of desperate.

It was at this point that Ruth showed initiative and went out to the fields to glean:

> And Ruth the Moabitess said to Naomi, "Let me go to the fields and pick up the leftover grain behind anyone in whose eyes I find favor." Naomi said to her, "Go ahead, my daughter." (Ruth 2:2)

The law allowed for poor people and aliens to do this. Landowners could harvest their crops by passing through their field or orchard once. Any fruit or vegetable that was missed or dropped was to be left for the less fortunate to gather. Landowners were also not to reap the corners of their fields. It was then the responsibility of the disadvantaged person to pick up what remained. The landowner did not have to expend his time and energy to make the ripe produce more readily available to the needy.

The legislation for gleaning is recorded in the books of Leviticus and Deuteronomy. Leviticus 19:9–10 says:

> When you reap the harvest of your land, do not reap to the very edges of your field or gather the gleanings of your harvest. Do not go over your vineyard a second time or pick up the grapes that have fallen. Leave them for the poor and the alien. I am the LORD your God.

And Leviticus 23:22, in the context of describing the Feast of Weeks, reinforces the earlier mandate:

> When you reap the harvest of your land, do not reap to the very edges of your field or gather the gleanings of your harvest. Leave them for the poor and the alien. I am the LORD your God.

Notice that both statements of the provision for gleaning are reinforced by the statement "I am the LORD your God."

Deuteronomy 24:19–22 adds even more force to the regulation by grounding it in the remembrance of the exodus:

> When you are harvesting in your field and you overlook a sheaf, do not go back to get it. Leave it for the alien, the fatherless and the widow, so that the LORD your God may bless you in all the work of your hands. When you beat the olives from your trees, do not go over the branches a second time. Leave what remains for the alien, the fatherless and the widow. When you harvest the grapes in your vineyard, do not go over the vines again. Leave what remains for the alien, the fatherless and the widow. Remember that you were slaves in Egypt. That is why I command you to do this.

Israelite landowners who left gleanings for the poor tangibly demonstrated an internalized understanding of what the LORD their God had done for his people in the exodus. As God had been kind and generous with the Israelites when Pharaoh oppressed them, so they in turn should beneficently treat the less fortunate in their midst.

Elsewhere in the Old Testament, Yahweh affirmed his protection of widows, orphans, and aliens, who were often more susceptible to deprivation and want. Compare the following verses:

> Do not take advantage of a widow or an orphan. If you do and they cry out to me, I will certainly hear their cry. My anger will be aroused, and I will kill you with the sword; your wives will become widows and your children fatherless. (Ex. 22:22–24)

> For the LORD your God is God of gods and Lord of lords, the great God, mighty and awesome, who shows no partiality and accepts no bribes. He defends the cause of the fatherless and the widow, and loves the alien, giving him food and clothing. And you are to love those who are aliens, for you yourselves were aliens in Egypt. (Deut. 10:17–19)

> The LORD watches over the alien and sustains the fatherless and the widow, but he frustrates the ways of the wicked. (Ps. 146:9)

Do not miss the parallelism in Psalm 146:9. If Yahweh is the subject of both verbs, the objects of both verbs are also related. The wicked in this context are those who oppress the disadvantaged and thereby demonstrate that they do not appreciate Yahweh's grace, especially as it was displayed during the exodus.

These charitable provisions of the law and the theology behind them reminded God's people of their unique status among the nations of the world. While everyone had to "make a living" and "put food on the table," making a living was not to consume the attention of God's people. One could work to meet his or her financial commitments and still not lose sight of ministering to others in Yahweh's name. The skeptic might say, "All man's efforts are for his mouth" (Eccl. 6:7), but the law instructed God's people to live for something bigger than personal consumption. Because God had provided manna in the wilderness, the Israelites had learned that "man does not live on bread alone but on every word that comes from the mouth of the LORD" (Deut. 8:3). God's provision for his people frees them to look out for the interests of others and thereby treat others as God has treated them.

Thus, economics had a missional outlook and so functioned as a "covenantal thermometer" to measure the vitality of Israel's love for God and neighbor.[2] When Israel enjoyed a right relationship with Yahweh, the social effects were justice and compassion among God's people. By contrast, any departure from a fervent trust in Yahweh and concomitant observance of his instruction correspondingly resulted in a seemingly unending list of social ills. "There was . . . an inseparable link between the kind of society Israel was (or was supposed to be) and the character of the God they worshipped."[3] What this means is that mission began at home as God's people ministered to one another. Godly social effects led, in turn, to outreach to those outside the covenant community. A healthy community would have the opportunity and mind-set to serve as a channel of God's redeeming grace to its unbelieving neighbors who could not help but notice the difference between a redeemed society on the one hand and their own painfully dysfunctional alternatives on the other.

Oppression, however, was always a possibility, especially during times of spiritual coldness. It is one thing to have laws and another to keep them. Other passages from later periods of apostasy and apathy indicted God's people for taking advantage of the less fortunate:

> Your rulers are rebels,
>   companions of thieves;
> they all love bribes
>   and chase after gifts.
> They do not defend the cause of the fatherless;
>   the widow's case does not come before them.
>   (Isa. 1:23)

Woe to those who make unjust laws,
    to those who issue oppressive decrees,
to deprive the poor of their rights
    and withhold justice from the oppressed of my
        people,
making widows their prey
    and robbing the fatherless. (Isa. 10:1–2)

So I will come near to you for judgment. I will be quick to testify against sorcerers, adulterers and perjurers, against those who defraud laborers of their wages, who oppress the widows and the fatherless, and deprive aliens of justice, but do not fear me," says the LORD Almighty. (Mal. 3:5)

They slay the widow and the alien;
    they murder the fatherless.
They say, "The LORD does not see;
    the God of Jacob pays no heed." (Ps. 94:6–7)

Sadly, these verses—and more could be listed—indicate that oppression of the defenseless was more than a possibility in Israel. All too often, it was the status quo.

Ruth hoped to find someone who would allow her on his property, but there were no guarantees. The law may have told God's people how to live as such, but it could not coerce godly conduct. Only the internal work of God's Spirit can transform a person's predisposition so that he or she willingly and cheerfully observes the commands of God. As events turned out, Ruth met not the owner of the field but his foreman who, in keeping with the law, allowed Ruth to glean in the field that had already been harvested.[4] When Boaz came later in the day, he exceeded the provision of the law by granting Ruth permission to pick grain alongside of Boaz's servant girls.

Something else to remember is Ruth's Moabite nationality. Deuteronomy 23:3–6 forbade friendship with Moabites because they were inhospitable to the tribes and even sought to do them harm. While an Israelite might have legal right to glean on another's property, a Moabite man or woman would not.[5] The next chapter will discuss Boaz's apparent disregard of Deuteronomy's legislation. For now, it is enough to note that Boaz rose above any charge of prejudice or xenophobia. He allowed Ruth to remain in his field when surely others would have chased her away. Even more remarkable, he assumed responsibility for her physical protection from those who might harm her because of nationality or gender. Why Boaz responded this way to Ruth's initiative will also be considered in the next chapter. For now, it is enough to note that God wanted his people to treat the disadvantaged in such ennobling ways.

THE FOUNDATION OF TRUST

Ruth 2:3 may initially offend theological sensibilities:

> So she went out and began to glean in the fields behind the harvesters. As it turned out, she found herself working in a field belonging to Boaz, who was from the clan of Elimelech.

In Hebrew, the words translated "as it turned out" are literally "her chance chanced." The sentence literally reads, "Her chance chanced the portion of the field belonging to Boaz." To capture the sense of the Hebrew, we could translate more idiomatically, "It just so happened that she found herself in a portion of the field that belonged to Boaz." The reference to blind chance is a brilliant rhetorical device that makes for good storytelling and good sermonizing. The writer did not believe in luck (Ruth 1:6; 4:13). Rather, he or she used this expression to get us thinking about the providential activity of God in the lives of Naomi and Ruth.[6]

Ruth's good fortune strains any belief in chance. From a human perspective, Ruth happened to glean in Boaz's field. She wandered into his field without intention or even knowledge. She could have just as unknowingly entered the field of the nearer kinsman (Ruth 3:12) or someone else. From God's perspective, though, Ruth was on Boaz's property by design. Everything that had happened to Naomi and Ruth over the last ten years had been foreordained by God to bring them to this moment. He was about to do something significant.

The "chance" wandering of Ruth onto Boaz's property is reinforced by what Naomi did not say in 2:2. When Ruth indicated her intention to glean in the field of "anyone in whose eyes I find favor," Naomi offered no suggestion as to where to inquire first. If Naomi, for whatever reason, said nothing about kinsmen and levirate marriage while she, Orpah, and Ruth were still in Moab, she again remained silent about advantageous possibilities. Being back home in Bethlehem had apparently not raised her hope for any familial solution to her (and Ruth's) destitution. The reader, therefore, cannot assign any credit to Naomi for Ruth's success in Boaz's field. Naomi's seemingly half-hearted consent to Ruth's initiative at the start of the day heightens the providential intervention of Yahweh later in the day.

Perhaps here is an appropriate place to respond to a dubious understanding of Ruth's words in Ruth 2:2. According to Jon L. Berquist, Ruth's expressed desire to find favor in the landowner's eyes had nothing to do with receiving permission to glean because the law already authorized Ruth to enter another person's field. Instead, suggests Berquist, Ruth wanted to use gleaning as an opportunity to catch the eye of a landowner and even seduce him into becoming her husband and provider.[7] Athalya Brenner's observation that Ruth "acts as a provider rather than looking for one" seems to reflect Ruth's motive more accurately.[8] It is obvious from Boaz's later words on the thresh-ing floor that Ruth did not try to use her feminine charms to attract a man—any man—as quickly as possible. At this point in the narrative, this godly woman wanted only to meet someone who would not chase her away. Eating, not marrying, was on her mind.

Ruth 2:3 builds on what the reader has been told in verse 1. While Boaz would not make his first appearance "on stage" until verse 4, verse 1 has already alerted the reader to his imminent involvement in Naomi and Ruth's predicament. In the dark days of the judges, there was still one "mighty man of valor." Though this expression often refers to a warrior, it may also denote a man of integrity and substance—hence, "man of standing" in the NIV. The Targum went so far as to translate with "a powerful man, strong in the Law."[9] While introducing Boaz as a Torah scholar might be too expanded of a reading, the Targum appreciably conveyed information about Boaz that becomes clearer throughout the remainder of the book—namely, that Boaz knew the law and followed it, even at personal cost. The biblical text further informs us that just as Ruth happened to wander into Boaz's field, so Boaz happened to be a relative of Elimelech. In the space of a few verses, the narrator hints that Naomi and Ruth's condition might not have been as hopeless as it first seemed. Ruth 2:1 and 2:3, together with Ruth 1:6, incline the reader to perceive that Naomi's belief in frowning providence will not have the last word in this story.

The lesson for all readers of Ruth is that God is work-ing behind the scenes to accomplish his purpose. Nothing occurs in our lives by randomness or chance. Seemingly small and insignificant decisions serve his purpose for our lives. We think nothing of day-to-day encounters, so-called accidents of history, but God uses ordinary events to advance his purpose. As suggested in Ruth 1:6 and through-out Ruth 2, that purpose is good. Even if the deaths of the men and the childlessness of the women signaled God's displeasure with this family (and the text does not explicitly say so), Ruth 1:6, 2:1, and 2:3 inform the reader that grace trumps justice. The books of Judges and Ruth share this same outlook on the judges period.

We might ask now about Naomi's awareness of Boaz. Ruth 2:1 tells us that Naomi's husband was survived by a relative named Boaz. Verse 20 indicates her knowledge of Boaz's familial connection. Why did Naomi not tell Ruth to glean in his field in verse 2? Several possibilities come to mind. Perhaps Naomi did not think that Ruth could "find her way around town." Maybe after ten years Naomi did not know where Boaz was or if he was alive. Boaz mentions a nearer kinsman in Ruth 3:12, and Naomi may have thought that any hope of help resided with him rather than Boaz. Why she did not say anything about the other man to Ruth is impossible to know. In Ruth 4 the nearer kinsman declines to perform the role of the redeemer. Naomi may have said nothing because no man was legally bound to marry his relative's widow, and she did not want to raise any false hope.[10] It was not until Boaz showed kindness in chapter 2 that Naomi tried to make something happen in chapter 3. Whatever the reason for Naomi's apparent silence about relatives, the writer emphasized the "chance" encounter of Ruth and Boaz. Even Naomi apparently never considered this possibility. God had, though.

Let us take stock of where we are. At the end of Ruth 1 and beginning of Ruth 2, Naomi and Ruth seemed to have no male provider or protector. By the end of chapter 2, they had grain to alleviate hunger for the short term. Midway through the book, then, there is movement from famine toward fullness. Not all concerns have been fully and finally addressed, but the tension has subsided enough to arouse hope. Unrelenting bleakness has given way to cautious optimism.

Similarly in the New Testament, Jesus, the incarnate Son of God, was rejected by everybody and unjustly put to death for claiming to be who he really is. Yet God was at work in the death of his Son to provide vicarious atonement for the sins of those who have faith in Jesus. In fact, God raised Jesus from the dead as proof of his satisfaction with his Son's expiatory work. Romans 4:25 says that Jesus "was raised to life for our justification." Throughout the Bible, bleak situations provide the stage for God's intervention in the lives of his people. We trust in a God who provided redemption in Jesus Christ when circumstances looked as if no redemption was possible. The events of our lives are the scene of his providential and redemptive activity. Nothing occurs by chance, takes God by surprise, or exceeds his power to handle. This is the foundation of trust.

THE LOOK OF TRUST

Now let us understand what it means to trust in the context of God's providential activity. Both Ruth and Boaz illustrate the look of trust. To trust a God of providence is to go above and beyond conventional wisdom. Ruth and Boaz responded to their different yet related circumstances in unusual ways.

In Ruth 1 Orpah and Naomi acted according to conventional wisdom. We would say that they acted practically and sensibly. They did nothing extraordinary so far as human decision-making is concerned. By contrast, Ruth committed herself to Yahweh, God of the Israelites, and remained loyal to her aging mother-in-law. At the beginning of Ruth 2, Ruth had already declared her faith in Naomi's covenant-keeping God and then put that faith into action. She, a younger woman and a foreign woman, took the risk of gleaning in the field of an unknown owner. Was she naïve, foolish, desperate, or actively trusting?

Meanwhile, Boaz enters the story for the first time. He is introduced as a man of substance and character. Both ideas are conveyed by the Hebrew wording that lies behind the NIV's "man of standing." Boaz is also said to be a relative of Elimelech. In 2:1 Ruth did not know any of this about Boaz. The information is given to the reader to arouse curiosity. Perhaps the barley harvest at the end of Ruth 1 was only the beginning of a brighter future for Naomi and Ruth. A well-to-do relative also existed nearby and might somehow factor into a turn of fortune.

The kindness that Boaz showed Ruth is extraordinary. He told Ruth to stay in his field. He allowed her to glean beside the women who were binding cut grain even though this part of the field was normally off limits to gleaners.[11] He gave Ruth access to the water supply. He instructed his workers not to disturb her and so protected her. He dined with her and sent the leftovers home with her.

Something else to note along this line is the vocabulary used of Ruth in chapter 2:

Boaz asked the foreman of his harvesters, "Whose young woman is that?" (Ruth 2:5)

So Boaz said to Ruth, "My daughter, listen to me. Don't go and glean in another field and don't go away from here. Stay here with my servant girls." (Ruth 2:8)

At this, she bowed down with her face to the ground. She exclaimed, "Why have I found such favor in your eyes that you notice me—a foreigner?" (Ruth 2:10)

"May I continue to find favor in your eyes, my lord," she said. "You have given me comfort and have spoken kindly to your servant—though I do not have the standing of one of your servant girls." (Ruth 2:13)

Whereas Ruth called herself a foreigner in 2:10 and said that she was not on the same level as Boaz' servant girls in verse 13, Boaz used the terms "young woman" in verse 5 and "my daughter" in verse 8. Rather than emphasizing the social distance between him and Ruth and so belittling her, he affirmed her personhood and elevated her standing in the group. This continues into chapter 3.[12]

Ruth's reaction helps us understand Boaz's magnanimity. She was astonished that the landowner would go so much beyond the requirement of the law. Surely Boaz's laborers observed and marveled too. If I might write anachronistically, the telephone lines in Bethlehem would have been burning up with gossip about these events of the day. Why would a man of substance and character risk his reputation on a Moabitess? Some have concluded that Boaz, who was in the stronger social position, had fallen in love with an attractive, though socially inferior, woman. His seemingly kind gestures supposedly had an ulterior and all-too-familiar motive.[13]

But did they really? If, as has been explained many times, Old Testament narratives make and develop their points through the speech of the characters, the prima facie meaning of Boaz and Ruth's conversation is consistent with how Boaz was introduced in Ruth 2:1, how he similarly described Ruth in Ruth 3:11, and how the women of Bethlehem praised God at the birth of Obed in Ruth 4:15. The human author and divine Author of the book do not want us to "read between the lines" and find double entendre and sexual innuendo that subversively cast doubt on the honor of Boaz and Ruth. Traditional or deconstructionist readers may want to consider Ruth a story of true love on the one hand or selfish desire on the other, but the author made no effort to emphasize romantic or flirtatious interest on the part of either Boaz or Ruth. The author told the story to get the reader thinking about divine providence and human loving-kindness. The speeches of Boaz and Ruth indicate that they were aware of both in their lives.

By the end of Ruth 2, even Naomi began to see the hand of God in the "chance" meeting of Ruth and Boaz:

> Her mother-in-law asked her, "Where did you glean today? Where did you work? Blessed be the man who took notice of you!"
>
> Then Ruth told her mother-in-law about the one at whose place she had been working. "The name of the man I worked with today is Boaz," she said.
>
> "The LORD bless him!" Naomi said to her daughter-in-law. "He has not stopped showing his kindness to the living and the dead." She added, "That man is our close relative; he is one of our kinsman-redeemers." (Ruth 2:19–20)

Naomi first blessed the man (Boaz) who made Ruth's gleaning more productive than would normally be expected and then invoked Yahweh's blessing on him. What follows next in the NIV is an ambiguous affirmation: "He has not stopped showing his kindness to the living and the dead." Is the antecedent of the pronoun "He" Boaz or Yahweh? The NIV's translation of the preceding clause ("The LORD bless him! Naomi said to her daughter-in-law") places the pronoun referring to Boaz (i.e., "him") closer to the pronoun "He" in the next clause (i.e., "He has not stopped showing his kindness"). The antecedent of "He" in the Hebrew text, however, is Yahweh. The whole sentence reads literally: "Naomi said to her daughter-law, 'May he [Boaz] be blessed by Yahweh who has not forsaken his kindness to the living and the dead.'" The Hebrew text removes all doubt that Naomi, who had earlier accused Yahweh of treating her malevolently, now saw the gracious hand of God in Ruth's "chance" encounter with Boaz that day. Back in Canaan, Naomi had observed in Ruth how good Yahweh could be to those who commit themselves to him, his people, and his land.

Yahweh's goodness, however, came through a member of the covenant community. Katharine Sakenfeld observes, "Divine loyalty takes shape in the community and in individual lives through human actions."[14] Put differently, God's grace has a human face. Boaz was more than a kind and gentle philanthropist. His first words in the book indicate his devotion to Israel's covenant God. His actions must be understood in view of covenantal grace. Because God had dealt graciously with him, he treated others similarly. He acknowledged Ruth's Gentile faith in Israel's covenant God and then ministered to her in the context of his own trust in Yahweh. Even so, Naomi properly recognized that Yahweh was the ultimate agent of blessing and that Boaz was the instrument. God had used faithful Boaz (and Ruth) to restore faithless Naomi to faith.

For Christians today, the human face of God's grace is, first of all, that of Jesus Christ. Though no sketch of his face exists, Jesus was God incarnate in Bethlehem and throughout Israel. In Jesus, we see how far God will go to reclaim and restore his people. Similar to Boaz, Jesus provided generous amounts of food for hungry people. Unlike Boaz, Jesus offered his own flesh and blood as spiritual food and drink to spiritually starving sinners. What Christians remember in the bread and the cup of the sacrament of the Lord's Supper is the self-sacrifice of the righteous Jesus for the sins of his unrighteous people. He absorbed in his body the penalty due us and so reconciled us to God whom our sins offended. Through Jesus Christ, God has blessed us not momentarily but eternally. If God's show of kindness through Boaz worked faith in Naomi, how much more does God's grace in the crucified and risen Jesus give believers today overwhelming evidence of God's good intention for his people?

This evidence should make a difference in how Christians face their daily circumstances. What God had done for Boaz made a difference in his life. He exhibited gratitude and trust that took the form of unconventional conduct. He reached out to a disadvantaged Moabitess with unprecedented generosity and seeming unconcern for personal reputation. For him, a life of trust took risks, that is, dared to love God and neighbor. The same is true for us who call ourselves followers of Jesus Christ. We become the face of a gracious God to all whom God brings across our path. Our displays of kindness to all manner of people proceed from the security that God grants his people in Jesus Christ. Because God has promised to provide for the needs of his people, we can dare to minister in his name to any and all who are made in his image.

We should note where a life of trust was lived in this book. Ruth and Boaz were not the movers and shakers of the ancient Near East. Yes, Boaz was a respected man of means, but he appears in no other ancient Near Eastern text. Secular history had no reason to remember him. In certain respects Boaz and Ruth were rather ordinary people in ordinary circumstances. The context of Ruth 2 is harvesting grain and putting food on the table. The larger context of Ruth 2 is the impoverishment of two widows in need of male protection. Some readers might disparage the book of Ruth for seemingly reinforcing female dependence on male patronage, but propagandizing for patriarchy is hardly the point of this book. A responsible reading of Ruth does not come away with more resentment over the battle between the sexes and greater determination to be assertive. Instead, it is humbled at and thrilled by how God redemptively used and uses the faithfulness of ordinary saints in a world that is not the way it is supposed to be. Once in a while, God advances his kingdom with a big splash on the stage of history, but, more often than not, he increases his glory through the quiet, persistent deeds of gratitude and kindness that never make the newspaper.

God providentially oversees the events of your life and so can be trusted. How can you go beyond conventional wisdom in the routine circumstances of your life and minister to others in Jesus' name? What holy risks can you take for the advancement of Christ's kingdom in your midst? That is the essence and look of trust.

FOR FURTHER REFLECTION

1. What does Ruth 2 teach about the relationship between human initiative and divine providence?
2. Can you recall an incident of "good chance" in your life that was simply too well-timed and too perfectly suited to be anything but the gracious hand of God intervening on your behalf?
3. Ruth and Boaz' example of trust and faithfulness began to make Naomi aware of another way of understanding God's activity in her life. Has God used another person's example of trust to open your eyes to the reality of his presence in your life? Has he used you to do the same for someone else?
4. Is there an area in your life where you are hesitant to entrust your well-being to God's care and risk ministering in the name of Jesus? How does Ruth 2 encourage you to walk by faith?
5. Boaz reached out to a Moabitess—someone different and even despised. Are there certain people whom you wish to avoid? Why?
6. What does Ruth 2 suggest about finding the will of God for your life?

5

UNDER GOD'S WINGS

When Ruth and Boaz met for the first time, she, as we saw in the previous chapter, experienced extraordinary kindness from him. Her reaction was understandably one of amazement and disbelief. In essence, she wondered why a prominent Israelite man would be so attentive and generous to her. Boaz then told Ruth what he had heard about her through the Bethlehem "grapevine." She had left her family in Moab to care for her mother-in-law and identify with the covenant people of God. He concluded with what must be called a prayer on her behalf: "May the LORD repay you for what you have done. May you be richly rewarded by the LORD, the God of Israel, under whose wings you have come to take refuge" (Ruth 2:12). In this chapter I want to look more closely at these words.

What Boaz says eases some of the tension that carries over from Ruth 1. While looking at Ruth 1, we referred to Deuteronomy 23:3–6. These verses forbade Moabites to enter the assembly of the Lord. In fact, the Israelites were told not to make a treaty of friendship with Moab. Perhaps Naomi did not want Orpah and Ruth to return with her for these reasons. They would never be welcome in Bethlehem, and neither would Naomi as long as she was associated with them. Modern readers may begin to feel uneasy not just with Naomi but also with the Old Testament. Did the Israelites feel that xenophobic, exclusive, even superior? Perhaps even more troubling, were they supposed to?

ISRAEL AS GOD'S ARMY

To some extent, the answer from earlier portions of Deuteronomy is yes. According to Deuteronomy 7, the Israelites were supposed to enter the Promised Land and eliminate the residents. Under no condition were the Israelites encouraged to marry the Canaanites or give their sons and daughters in marriage to them. The stated reason for this policy of intolerance is that the Canaanites would draw the Israelites away from unalloyed devotion to Yahweh:

> Do not intermarry with them. Do not give your daughters to their sons or take their daughters for your sons, for they will turn your sons away from following me to serve other gods, and the LORD's anger will burn against you and will quickly destroy you. (Deut. 7:3–4)

The implication of Deuteronomy 7:4 is stated explicitly in Deuteronomy 9:4–6 and 20:17–18:

> After the LORD your God has driven them out before you, do not say to yourself, "The LORD has brought me here to take possession of this land because of my righteousness." No, it is on account of the wickedness of these nations that the LORD is going to drive them out before you. It is not because of your righteousness or your integrity that you are going in to take possession of their land; but on account of the wickedness of these nations, the LORD your God will

drive them out before you, to accomplish what he swore to your fathers, to Abraham, Isaac and Jacob. Understand, then, that it is not because of your righteousness that the LORD your God is giving you this good land to possess, for you are a stiff-necked people. (Deut. 9:4–6)

Completely destroy them—the Hittites, Amorites, Canaanites, Perizzites, Hivites and Jebusites—as the LORD your God has commanded you. Otherwise, they will teach you to follow all the detestable things they do in worshiping their gods, and you will sin against the LORD your God. (Deut. 20:17–18)

The Israelites were not able to withstand the temptations of Canaanite theology and culture. God's people innately possessed neither moral superiority that had commended them to God's favor nor moral backbone that would resist the allurements of the Canaanites. Rather, God had chosen to set his affection on Israel in spite of their proclivity to act like anyone else, and he would use his people, already redeemed but not yet fully sanctified, to bring redemptive blessing to others. For now, though, they were to concentrate on keeping themselves pure before God and administer judgment against the Canaanites, whose cup of iniquity had filled up (Deut. 9:4; cf. Gen. 15:16).

The concern about the seduction of Canaanite culture in Deuteronomy 20:18 occurs within the context of rules for holy war. These rules presupposed what the book of Numbers said about Israel as God's army.[1] After constituting the tribes as a holy people and kingdom of priests in Exodus 19:6 and giving the law in Exodus 19–23 to instruct his people how to perform these roles, Yahweh additionally commissioned all males over twenty years of age (Levites excepted) to serve in the military. A census in Numbers 1 counted the men eligible for duty. Numbers 2 records how the tribes set up camp in a specific configuration that kept battle divisions together so as to facilitate orderly deployment. At the beginning of Numbers, Israel had the appearance and discipline of a well-trained army. All of this preparation anticipated the fulfillment of Genesis 15:13–16:

> Then the LORD said to [Abraham], "Know for certain that your descendants will be strangers in a country not their own, and they will be enslaved and mistreated four hundred years. But I will punish the nation they serve as slaves, and afterward they will come out with great possessions. You, however, will go to your fathers in peace and be buried at a good old age. In the fourth generation your descendants will come back here, for the sin of the Amorites has not yet reached full measure."

Abraham's descendants would go into Egypt, and then God would bring them to Canaan so that they might serve as his agent of judgment against the Canaanites.

Of note, though, is the erection of the tabernacle in the center of the Israelite camp (Num. 2). The centrality of the tabernacle emphasized the sacred nature of Israel's warfare. Israel would not succeed at war because of superior weaponry or strategy. Rather, sin could undercut any advantage that strength and cunning might otherwise bring. Ritual purity and covenantal exactitude would prevent the mission from being sabotaged from within the ranks of Israel's army and assure that Yahweh, the Divine Warrior, would lead his army to victory. So then, Israel's true weapon was a redeemed disposition submissive to Yahweh.

Numbers actually tells the story of two generations of soldiers. The first came out of Egypt but failed to remain faithful. Soon after being deployed in Numbers 10, the first generation began to complain about the menu and then shrank back from the mission upon hearing the report of the spies in Numbers 13. Yahweh forbade that generation from entering the Promised Land and condemned them to wander around the desert until all but Joshua and Caleb died. The last 24,000 perished in a plague sent to punish them for immorality with Moabite women and worship of Moabite gods:

> While Israel was staying in Shittim, the men began to indulge in sexual immorality with Moabite women, who invited them to the sacrifices to their gods. The people ate and bowed down before these gods. So Israel joined in worshiping the Baal of Peor. And the LORD's anger burned against them. . . . [And] those who died in the plague numbered 24,000. (Num. 25:1–3, 9)

Thomas W. Mann insightfully observes, "The greatest threat in that passage is not the *armies* of the peoples, but rather their religion and culture."[2] These operated more insidiously so that Moab could defeat Israel without ever having to throw a spear or brandish a sword.

It should be noted that the Moabites were not Canaanites, that is, residents of Canaan. Neither Genesis 15:19–21 nor Deuteronomy 7:1 included the Moabites in the list of peoples to be dispossessed by the army of Israel. In fact, Deuteronomy 2:9 recalls Yahweh's earlier instruction to Moses not to make war with Moab. This directive changed, however, when the Moabites and Midianites turned hostile toward Israel—first by hiring Balaam to pronounce curses against Israel and second by seducing Israel to indulge in sexual immorality and false worship. Yahweh later told Moses, "Take vengeance on the Midianites for the Israelites" (Num. 31:2). The Moabites had, in effect, become like the Canaanites by their abominable religion and conduct that threatened God's purpose for Israel.

The second generation then received the same commission as its parents (Num. 26) and happily gave evidence that it had learned from its parents' mistakes. Even so, the book of Numbers has an open-ended conclusion. The story of the second generation in Numbers ends on the east side of the Jordan River and does not report the entrance into Canaan. The second generation exemplified the life of faith and obedience for each succeeding generation that similarly awaits the realization of God's promised rest.

If, then, Israel was supposed to maintain moral and cultic purity as well as eliminate the Canaanites, it should be pointed out that the basis for separation was theological, not national or racial.[3] God wanted his people to remain distinct from the nations so that ultimately they might minister a message of grace to them. As well as being God's army, Israel was a kingdom of priests. That the Canaanites had exhausted divine patience and were about to be confirmed in their depravity does not detract from the redemptive mission that Israel had to others. While humans may not fully comprehend the relationship between God's justice and grace, the Bible maintains that God is both just and gracious. For his grace to be revealed through the Israelites, though, they had to present a distinct lifestyle that modeled the attractive benefits of being in relationship with Yahweh.

This redemptive mission, in fact, nuances the commands to destroy the Canaanites. Deuteronomy 7:2 and 20:17 called for total destruction of the Canaanites by Joshua and the army of Israel. Yet, the spies that Joshua sent out in Joshua 2 promised to spare Rahab and her family because she testified to her faith in Yahweh and protected them. Neither the book of Joshua nor Joshua the person disapproved of their agreement with her, and Joshua 6:25 records the sparing of Rahab and her family. Moreover, Hebrews 11:31 holds up Rahab as an example of faith. She is distinguished from those who were disobedient. Similarly, James 2:25 calls her righteous because she helped the spies at potential risk to her life. Rahab's confession of faith made the difference, and her confession was based on the mighty deeds of God. She had heard what God had done for his people for the last forty years, and she knew that God would give Canaan to the tribes. God used the reports of his activity to bring this Gentile woman to faith. There was a place in the covenant community for her.

But let us go back even farther in time. Exodus 12:38 reports that other people left Egypt with the tribes. These folks were Egyptians or other foreigners who believed in Yahweh. Presumably God had used the plagues to bring them to faith (see Ex. 9:20). They had put blood on the doorpost as evidence of their belief in the word of God through his prophet Moses. Exodus similarly indicates that there was a place for them among God's people.

The Pentateuch goes back even farther than the exodus to the call of Abraham. Deuteronomy 26:5 remembers Abraham as "a wandering Aramean," who, according to Genesis 11:31, lived in Ur of the Chaldeans. Joshua 24:2 adds that Abraham's father worshiped other gods. In theological terms, Abraham was not "a child of the covenant," "a cradle Episcopalian," or one who "grew up in a Christian home." God sovereignly called this pagan to faith as an adult.

It is fair to say, then, that no one belongs to God's people because of birth. Being a child of God comes about by new birth. Jesus made the same point with Nicodemus (John 3:3), who surely was a circumcised Israelite and a "member of the visible church." Regeneration involves faith in the promises of God, and faith starts with knowledge of the redemptive acts of God. Old Testament saints believed God's promises regarding vicarious atonement through the blood of lambs. Followers of Jesus Christ today trust in the blood of the Lamb who takes away the sin of the world. According to the book of Hebrews, the sacrifices of the Old Testament anticipated and typified Christ's definitive and final sacrifice for sin:

> Then Christ would have had to suffer many times since the creation of the world. But now he has appeared once for all at the end of the ages to do away with sin by the sacrifice of himself. Just as man is destined to die once, and after that to face judgment, so Christ was sacrificed once to take away the sins of many people; and he will appear a second time, not to bear sin, but to bring salvation to those who are waiting for him. (Heb. 9:26–28)

Theologians speak of the active and passive obedience of Jesus. These technical terms have to do with what Jesus accomplished for believers through his life and death. The New Testament scholar Martin Kähler said that the Gospels are "passion narratives with extended introductions."[4] This observation is theologically problematic because it seems to miss the importance of Jesus' life. It is no small matter that Jesus lived a sinless life. He did what no other human has done, namely, keep the law of God. Everyone else has fallen short of God's standard and so justly incurred the judgment of God. Still, the standard exists, and God requires untarnished obedience. We might even dare to say that salvation has always been by works. Someone has to keep the law. The good news of the gospel is that Jesus has perfectly kept the law—what is called active obedience. Because Jesus is the second Adam and as such the representative of a new race of redeemed humanity, his obedience is imputed to those who believe in him.

For a complete gospel, though, the active obedience necessitates the passive obedience. Here the word "passive" does not mean idle or submissive. Instead, it has to do with Jesus' passion—his suffering and death. In fact, Philippians 2:8 speaks of Jesus' obedience unto death. By suffering and dying for our sins, Jesus bore the penalty for our sins. In life, then, Jesus fully obeyed the revealed will of God, and his righteousness is imputed to those who believe in Jesus. In death, Jesus had our unrighteousness imputed to him. If trust is only as good as its object, saving trust is directed at the sinless Son of God who loved his people and gave himself for them.

Saving trust not only affirms Jesus' active and passive obedience but also shows regard for Jesus' commands. We do not trust God to give us what we want. Rather, we trust him to accomplish his redemptive plan and evidence that trust by doing his will in the situations of our lives. Let us return to Exodus for a moment. Although Exodus does not say, it is conceivable that some Israelites did not put blood on the doorpost and thereby signified their lack of faith and their unwillingness to obey the prophet, Moses. Jesus would later call some Jews children of the devil (John 8:44). Paul would say that not all Israel is Israel and not all of Abraham's descendants are his children (Rom. 9:6–7). Faith in the blood of the Lamb is the prerequisite for membership among the people of God.[5] It is then evidenced by obedience to God's revealed will. Faith in anything else represents pride and self-sufficiency.

The point of this digression is that readers of the Old Testament must not confuse xenophobia and covenantal faithfulness. Anyone could hear of Yahweh's mighty deeds and put his or her faith in the self-revealing, covenant-making God of Israel. The "free offer of the gospel" was valid for all, Jew or Gentile. At the same time, the covenant community was a community in covenant with Yahweh. The relationship included historical knowledge of how God had redeemed his people and instruction on how a redeemed people should live as such for the glory of God, the enrichment of one another, and the "evangelization" of others.

Any threats to the covenantal relationship, from within the community or without, had to be removed for the benefit of the members as well as those who were yet to become members through the witness of the community.

BOAZ'S ACCEPTANCE OF RUTH

Getting back to Ruth 2, Boaz did not seem to be the least bit disturbed by Ruth's nationality. He certainly knew from where she came. The whole town appeared to be up to the minute with the news of Naomi's return. Why, though, was Boaz so friendly to Ruth? Did he not know about Deuteronomy 23, or was he lax in his application of Scripture? Either option was possible in the apostate days of the judges. In actuality, though, neither option accounts for Boaz's words. Rather, a good understanding of God's Word lay behind them.

In Ruth (the person) Boaz saw just the opposite of a threat. Ruth had given up everything and had cast herself completely on the God of Israel. While she might not have been a blood descendant of Abraham, her faith had the same object as his. As Abraham had left his family behind in Haran, so Ruth had recently separated herself from the Moabites and identified with God's people. Here is the essence of holiness to which God's people are called: forsaking impurity in all its forms and committing one's time, talent, and resources to the service of God. Moreover, Ruth upheld the law by showing kindness to disadvantaged Naomi. She had done all this because of her trust in the God of Israel.

What this means is that Deuteronomy had been upheld, and Boaz knew it. Boaz properly regarded Ruth as a member of the covenant community. She was no foreigner barred from the assembly of God's people. The Old Testament never called for ethnic or racial separation per se. Its standard for separation was theological. God's people could not mix the tenets and practices of incompatible world-views, and Ruth was not trying to do so. She had committed herself unreservedly to the content of Israel's faith, and her actions indicated her continuation in a true profession. Perhaps we may explicitly make a connection with what comes later in the book. Once Ruth confessed her faith in Yahweh, "no obstacle . . . existed any longer for an Israelite to marry her."[6]

Murray Gow notes how Ruth 2 begins to incorporate Ruth into her new identity. While 2:2, 6, and 21 still refer to Ruth as a Moabitess, *everywhere there is a movement for her inclusion.*[7] Naomi and Boaz separately address Ruth as "my daughter" (2:2, 8, 22). Ruth is also called Naomi's daughter-in-law. Naomi says that Boaz is "our relative" and one of "our redeemers." Boaz invites Ruth to come back to his field and takes responsibility for her protection and care. He further allows Ruth to participate in the harvest as far more than a gleaner. In fact, Boaz tells Ruth to "stay here with" (NIV) his servant girls. The Hebrew verb is the same one that appears in 1:14 and is translated "clung." Ruth now belongs in this new place with these members of the covenant community. She has put off a former way of life and put on the new way of God's covenant.

Boaz was confident, then, that Ruth would receive the blessing of God, and his prayer in Ruth 2:12 expressed this conviction. He invoked Yahweh, the God of Israel, to "repay" and "reward" Ruth "for what you have done." The English words "repay" and "reward" may give a misleading impression. We should not think of obligatory remuneration for services rendered. Faith in God does not reduce to a contractual arrangement. Boaz was not attributing Ruth's exemplary conduct to a give-to-get strategy: she trusted and obeyed God to give her what she wanted. God, then, would not have been the true object of her affection. Rather, he would have supplied the object of her affection after receiving the fee of her obedience. Nor was Boaz saying that Ruth deserved something because of all that she had endured. God was not "'mak[ing] up what is due' to Ruth for all the pain she has suffered in her self-giving to Naomi."[8] Ruth did not "deserve a break today," and God did not "owe her one."

The words "repay" and "richly" come from the same root from which Hebrew gets *shalom*. The root has to do with completion or wholeness. Ruth 2:12 could be translated as follows: "May Yahweh finish your work, and may your wages be complete from Yahweh God of Israel under whose wings you have come to seek refuge." The word "wages" must be a metaphor because God did not literally remunerate Ruth with a paycheck. What Boaz affirmed is that provision in this life and inheritance in the next are involved with a relationship with Yahweh because they are part of the salvation package—what Paul calls "the riches of God's grace" (Eph. 1:7).

Philippians 1:6, 1 Corinthians 15:58, and Ephesians 2:10 get at the theological sense of Ruth 2:12:

> In all my prayers for all of you, I always pray with joy . . . being confident of this, that he who began a good work in you will carry it on to completion until the day of Christ Jesus. (Phil. 1:4, 6)

> Therefore, my dear brothers, stand firm. Let nothing move you. Always give yourselves fully to the work of the Lord, because you know that your labor in the Lord is not in vain. (1 Cor. 15:58)

> For we are God's workmanship, created in Christ Jesus to do good works, which God prepared in advance for us to do. (Eph. 2:10)

Boaz expressed hope that God would finish the good work that he had sovereignly and graciously begun in Ruth (Phil.

1:6) and so redeem the labor of her hands (1 Cor. 15:58). Both Yahweh and Ruth were partners in Yahweh's will for Ruth's life. God had made promises that he was covenantally obligated to fulfill, and Ruth had done the good works that God had prepared in advance for her to do (Eph. 2:10). That God's regenerating and sanctifying grace made Ruth's change of heart and lifestyle possible does not discount the fact that Ruth willingly and cheerfully acted like a redeemed child of God.[9] In short, Boaz was reminding Ruth of the benefits of salvation. She could know that God would take care of her because security was part of the covenant.

How beautifully Boaz expressed the assurance of God's care. Ruth had come to take refuge under Yahweh's wings. This expression is found in several psalms:

> Both high and low among men
> find refuge in the shadow of your wings.
> (Ps. 36:7)

> Have mercy on me, O God, have mercy on me,
> for in you my soul takes refuge.
> I will take refuge in the shadow of your wings
> until the disaster has passed. (Ps. 57:1)

> I long to dwell in your tent forever
> and take refuge in the shelter of your wings.
> (Ps. 61:4)

> He will cover you with his feathers,
> and under his wings you will find refuge;
> his faithfulness will be your shield and rampart.
> (Ps. 91:4)

The verb "to take refuge" is found numerous other times in the Psalms, as are references to God's wings. In

Psalm 17:7–8, "to take refuge" and "wings" are not in the same clause but are in close proximity to one another:

> Show the wonder of your great love,
>> you who save by your right hand
>> those who take refuge in you from their foes.
> Keep me as the apple of your eye;
>> hide me in the shadow of your wings
> from the wicked who assail me,
>> from my mortal enemies who surround me.

Most of the psalms in which these terms appear are psalms of lament. In them, the psalmist prayed about some indefinitely expressed threat to his well-being as a servant of God and pleaded for deliverance so that God's redemptive program, of which he was a part, might advance. Other psalms (e.g., Ps. 18:30; 34:8) are thanksgiving songs that recall an earlier lament and express gratitude for deliverance.

What, then, was Boaz trying to communicate in Ruth 2:12? As young, weak, and helpless chicks find protection from predators (cf. Ps. 7:1–2, 57:1–4) and the elements (cf. Ps. 91:1–6) under the wings of the mother bird, so Ruth, against whom life had thrown some of the worst that it has to offer, had by faith become a recipient of God's metaphors of security. The idea, of course, is that God is faithful and therefore trustworthy. He does not renege on his promises. He is great enough to perform what he says he will do. He is good enough to want to perform what he says he will do.

Moreover, it is fair to say that Ruth embodied an implication of the laments. Laments assume human limitation. We humans are not able to gain life, security, or even goodness on our own. Because of the effects of the fall on creation and other people (enemies without), as well as the believer's own struggle with his or her sinful nature (enemies within), it is foolish for humans, including God's people, to imagine that they are self-sufficient. God does not help those who help themselves. Rather, he helps those who cannot help themselves, know it, and rely on him. While it is true that Ruth was exerting effort to glean, she had expressed her dependence on a landowner to allow her onto his property (Ruth 2:2), and behind that expression lay an awareness of the provision of God's law for the needy. Ruth was acting on the Word of God and trusting him to oversee the variables (her work, the landowner's kindness) that factored into the alleviation of her and Naomi's hunger. Ruth may have been quite energetic in chapter 2, but her initiative in going out to glean must be balanced by Boaz's acknowledgement of her humility and trust. The explanation for her activity was her deep faith in Yahweh.

Our assurance of God's faithfulness depends on the mighty acts of God in history that accomplish our redemption, and the mightiest is the death and resurrection of Jesus Christ. If God has acted in Jesus to atone for our sins and reconcile us to himself, then he will surely follow through on the rest of his promises. In Christ we know that God has not brought us this far to forget about us. He will see his redemptive plan through to completion and wholeness.

If we might look ahead to Ruth 3, what Boaz did not seem to realize yet was how much he would be the answer to his prayer for Ruth. To this point, his prayer was not hollow for he sent Ruth home with a truly generous amount of grain. According to Ruth 2:17, Ruth took an ephah, or about thirty pounds, of threshed barley back to Naomi. As seen by Naomi's reaction to the quantity of one day's work, the famine was over and the food pantry was full. Even so, the harvest would not last forever, and these women would eventually consume the grain. They would, in time, need a more permanent solution to their situation. Ruth 3 will bring some surprises.

FOR FURTHER REFLECTION

1. How is Christianity exclusive? How is it inclusive? What are some abuses of both realities?
2. What would you say is the church's mission, and how is the image of a holy army appropriate for that mission? Can you relate Numbers' understanding of a holy army that does not rely on superior weaponry or strategy to your local church?
3. What are some indirect and even insidious threats to the accomplishments of the church's mission?
4. If Deuteronomy 23:3–6 forbade a treaty of friendship between Israel and Moab, on what basis did Boaz welcome Ruth onto his property and into the covenant community?
5. Explain the basis of the believer's assurance that God will be a refuge for his people.

6

OF ALL THAT COULD
HAVE GONE WRONG

It is probably fair to say that most readers of the book of Ruth consider it a heartwarming love story. Even in scholarly books and articles on Ruth, one can readily find affirmations of the attraction that Boaz and Ruth felt toward each other. Such inferences, however, lack explicit textual support. The book of Ruth says nothing about Ruth's physical appearance, though Boaz's reference to younger men in Ruth 3:10 gives the impression that younger men would take an interest in her. Still, there is no explicit indication that Boaz and Ruth "fell in love." Whatever truth there is to the popular assessment (and I am not ready to give up on it completely), Ruth 3 would certainly prevent a movie on the traditional reading of the book from receiving a G rating. Here is mature content that requires parental guidance for younger children.

A discussion of Ruth 3 could be given several titles. For reasons that will become clearer, I have selected "Of All That Could Have Gone Wrong." Perhaps another title could be "It Worked!" or "What Really Happened That Night?" What Naomi cooked up for Ruth here was fraught with potential disaster. This chapter is full of double entendre and provocative suggestion. Nevertheless, God continued to work behind the scenes to accomplish his good plan.

This chapter offers hope to you and me. Our lives are not squeaky clean, and we can find ourselves in real jams—sometimes of our own doing and sometimes of someone else's. At times, we don't know what the right thing to do is. A situation calls for a decision, and we make one. Here we learn the truth of Romans 8:28 that "in all things God works for the good of those who love him." Let us start with the disastrous possibilities of Naomi's scheme.

NOT THE BRIGHTEST IDEA

We should give Naomi credit for wanting to find a husband for Ruth. Whatever Naomi may have thought about the possibility of levirate marriage while still in Moab, Boaz's recent kindness and generosity must have raised her hopes. In Ruth 2:20 she said that Boaz was a kinsman-redeemer—a term that will be further explained in the next chapter. It is hard not to think that the wheels were turning inside Naomi's head, and who could blame her after all that she had endured? Still, any hope of quick nuptials seems to have ended in disappointment. According to Ruth 2:23, Ruth continued to glean in Boaz's field until the end of the barley and wheat harvests. This statement suggests that some time—perhaps as many as seven weeks (cf. Deut. 16:9)—had passed between the initial meeting of Ruth and Boaz in chapter 2 and the nocturnal meeting in chapter 3. The text does not say if Ruth and Boaz continued to have regular contact, though it is hard to imagine that they did not.

Given that Naomi arranged an irregular meeting between the two, she must have started to wonder if nothing more than food for the short term would come from such a promising encounter that first day in Boaz's field. Was Boaz not attracted to Ruth? Was he married to someone else with whom he had children and so hesitated to get any more involved? Was he deferring to the nearer kinsman? The text does not say.

Naomi apparently waited as long as she thought that she could and then decided to try to make something happen. She told Ruth to bathe, dress, and go to the threshing floor where Boaz would spend the night winnowing his grain. We should not think that Ruth was "dressed to kill." She bathed and perfumed herself because she had most likely been gleaning in the field all day. The Hebrew word translated "best clothes" in the NIV does not necessarily mean anything more than an outer garment that would keep Ruth warm in the evening air.[1] The word is used in Exodus 22:26–27 of a poor person's cloak that should be returned in the evening for sleeping. Perhaps Ruth used it to carry home the grain in the early hours of the morning (Ruth 3:15). Before Ruth departed for the threshing floor, Naomi offered instructions for approaching Boaz and learning his intentions.

Let us be honest about Naomi's scheme. Approaching Boaz on the threshing floor was not a prudent idea. Naomi put Ruth in real danger. Because threshing floors lay outside the town, Ruth could have been abducted on the way and never made it to Boaz. Boaz could have taken offense at Ruth's forwardness and refused to have anything more to do with her. Though a man of standing in the community, he could have taken advantage of Ruth, and, if necessary, lied about what happened. Who would have believed Ruth's side of the story, and would Naomi have publicly defended her Moabite daughter-in-law? Robert L. Hubbard Jr., asks, "Would such feminine forwardness flatter, embarrass, or anger [Boaz]?"[2] There was simply no guarantee that he would respond favorably or honorably. Also, someone could have awakened and seen Ruth at Boaz's feet. In the unsavory days of the judges, prostitutes would offer their services at such places (cf. Hos. 9:1). If people are people no matter when and where they live, the Bethlehemites would have savored a sex scandal. Naomi did no one any favor that night. She put both Ruth and Boaz at risk of yielding to temptation or being unjustly accused.

What Ruth thought about Naomi's scheme and why she went ahead with it cannot be known. The text merely reports her assent and compliance. The author of Ruth was not an omniscient narrator who knew people's private thoughts. He or she tells us that Ruth went to the threshing floor, waited until the right moment, uncovered Boaz, and lay down. The sparseness of detail does not correspond with the overload of suggestiveness. Who can but wonder what happened on that threshing floor? Some say that Ruth and Boaz had sexual intercourse. Others say no.

The language certainly connotes an unseemly situation. First, Ruth uncovered Boaz's feet. In Hebrew, the word "uncover" is used especially in Leviticus 18 (multiple times), Ezekiel 16:37, and Ezekiel 23:10 with reference to uncovering nakedness or exposing the genitals for illicit sexual relations:

No one is to approach any close relative to have sexual relations [literally, uncover the nakedness]. I am the LORD. (Lev. 18:6)

Therefore I am going to gather all your lovers, with whom you found pleasure, those you loved as well as those you hated. I will gather them against you from all around and will strip you [literally, uncover your nakedness] in front of them, and they will see all your nakedness. (Ezek. 16:37)

They stripped her naked [literally, uncovered her nakedness], took away her sons and daughters and killed her with the sword. She became a byword among women, and punishment was inflicted on her. (Ezek. 23:10)

Second, the word *feet* can serve as a euphemism for relieving oneself (1 Sam. 24:3), shaving pubic hair to shame prisoners of war (Isa. 7:20), or committing adultery (Ezek. 16:25):

> He came to the sheep pens along the way; a cave was there, and Saul went in to relieve himself [literally, cover his feet]. David and his men were far back in the cave. (1 Sam. 24:3)

> In that day the Lord will use a razor hired from beyond the River—the king of Assyria—to shave your head and the hair of your legs [literally, feet], and to take off your beards also. (Isa. 7:20)

> At the head of every street you built your lofty shrines and degraded your beauty, offering your body [literally, opened your feet] with increasing promiscuity to anyone who passed. (Ezek. 16:25)

In each of these euphemistic uses of "feet," the genitals are exposed for others to see. Third, Ruth lay down at Boaz's feet. While lying at someone's feet might signal humility and probably did in Ruth's case, the verb "lie" often connotes sexual intercourse:

> The next day the older daughter said to the younger, "Last night I lay with my father. Let's get him to drink wine again tonight, and you go in and lie with him so we can preserve our family line through our father." (Gen. 19:34)

> But if out in the country a man happens to meet a girl pledged to be married and rapes her [literally,

seizes her and lies with her], only the man who has done this will die. (Deut. 22:25)

The appearance of these three terms—"uncover," "feet," and "lie"—in the context of a nocturnal meeting of a man and woman charges this encounter with sexual innuendo.

Furthermore, the whole scene in Ruth 3 evokes a nervous sense of déjà vu, though it is impossible to know if Boaz would have made the following connection on the spot. As was said earlier, Moab does not have the best reputation in the Old Testament. According to Genesis 19:37, Moab was originally the name given by Lot's older daughter to the son that she had with her drunken father. Ruth, of course, was a Moabitess lying down next to a man who had drunk some wine. While Boaz may not have been "smashed" (and his lucid comments after being awakened would suggest that he was not), readers who make the connection with Genesis 19 cannot help but wonder how this later scene compares with the former one.[3]

How much, then, of Boaz's lower body did Ruth uncover, and where did she lie? The complicating factor in Ruth 3 is that the word for "feet" is not the same word that occurs, say, in Ezekiel 16:25. *Regel*, the standard word for "foot," occurs there, but *margelot* in Ruth 3. The latter is derived from the former and does not appear nearly as often in the Old Testament. The less frequent word occurs four times in Ruth 3 and once in Daniel 10:6, where it is used in tandem with "arms" and so is best translated "legs":

> His body was like chrysolite, his face like lightning, his eyes like flaming torches, his arms and legs like the gleam of burnished bronze, and his voice like the sound of a multitude. (Dan. 10:6)

Though the opening verses of Ruth 3 are rich with double entendre and prurient echoes, it is still reasonable to say that Ruth uncovered Boaz's legs, lay down beside him, and waited for him to awaken. It was the cool night air and not Ruth's warm body that startled Boaz. He most likely discovered her at his feet when he groggily sat up to cover his exposed legs. Ruth and Boaz, then, did not commit fornication. The suggestive language, however, helps us understand how difficult this context was for them. There was real temptation and awkwardness. How much stronger was the temptation if the traditional reading of the book is correct, namely, that Ruth and Boaz were already attracted to one another? One can only wonder if Ruth did not have more to say to Naomi than is recorded in Ruth 3:16–17— perhaps something like "What were you thinking?!" It was Naomi, after all, who got Ruth into that potentially compromising situation.

Further evidence of Ruth and Boaz's integrity is found in how Boaz described Ruth in Ruth 3:11. As he was described as a man of character in 2:1, so he said that she was a woman of character in 3:11. If they had fornicated, 3:11 with its recollection of 2:1 makes no sense. First, an honorable man and an honorable woman who are not married to each other do not have sexual intercourse in an out-of-the-way location and then tell each other how honorable they are. Second, Boaz would have usurped the right of the nearer kinsman, something that he was expressly unwilling to do.[4] Here, then, were two godly people in a most unusual setting not entirely of their making, and they handled it with integrity to the glory of God and, as the rest of the book will show, the eventual blessing of God's people.[5]

A GOD OF AWKWARD MOMENTS

So then, what does Ruth 3 mean for God's people today? We may not winnow grain at night in Israel and find ourselves alone with someone else on a threshing floor, but it is fair to say that our lives do not proceed in a neat, cut-and-dried fashion. Life is not squeaky clean, and God lets it be that way for now.

We sometimes look at other people's decisions and make judgments. Too often, we think that we know what other people should do, or what we would do if we were in their shoes. Then we rush to criticize them or gossip about them. Sooner or later, though, we find ourselves in a situation where right and wrong are not so clear or the way out of wrong and back to right is blurry. Every choice may seem to be a mixture of good and bad, and we hope that others will not make simplistic, uninformed judgments about us. What might some of these morally dubious moments be?

After I graduated from college and was trying to earn money for seminary, I approached a man in the church that I attended and asked about working for him. This man, a respected elder in the church, was the sales manager for a car dealership. In response to my request, he said something like the following, "Dean, selling cars is a dirty business, and I am good at it. I hate to see someone preparing for pastoral ministry get mixed up in this line of work." Even so, he made a living at auto sales, and I do not doubt that he maintained integrity. Still, his concern for me undoubtedly said something about the tension in his own life. How many believers have an immoral boss who pushes the bottom line and does not care how employees pressure customers, just so they clinch the deal?

When I went to seminary, a fellow student recalled in a sermon on Proverbs 7 how he and his wife were on a tour of Amsterdam and the guide asked who would be interested in seeing the red light district. All hands but two went up. Because my fellow seminarian and his wife did not know their way around Amsterdam, they stayed with the group and got an eyeful. Had they known ahead of time about the "added bonus," they may not have taken the tour, but being in the wrong place at the wrong time has a way of catching people off guard.

Often we vote for the least objectionable candidate, or we go to Christmas parties and other dubious social occasions. When my wife, daughter, and I were invited to our next-door neighbor's birthday party, we enjoyed ourselves until Carla the Clown showed up with her assortment of raunchy jokes and sexual toys. While the humor thankfully went over my daughter's head, my wife and I could not decide whether to stay or walk across the imaginary property line to the safe haven of our yard. We decided to stay because, long after Carla the Clown packed up her brand of adult entertainment, we would still be neighbors of the birthday boy—and his wife who had booked Carla the Clown.

Some people might think that the answer is to go into the ministry and find insulation from a world that is not the way it is supposed to be. I have been in pastoral ministry and know that the church is full of moral dilemmas. I have been caught in the middle of a complex web of power plays and seething resentment. People were involved at all levels of culpability, and every solution seemed in its own way to compound the evil. There was no obvious way to untangle all the strands and set everything right. By no means does the ministry exempt one from moral conundrums.

The answer, then, is not to go into the ministry. Besides, followers of Jesus Christ, whether ordained or lay, are already in the ministry and are to reach out to one another and to unbelievers. When ministering to people, there is always a history of sin and its deleterious effects. Those who serve others in Jesus' name cannot avoid getting their hands dirty. They surely have times of confusion and make mistakes.

We cannot control all of life's variables, and God knows this. The answer is to appeal to God's grace in Jesus Christ, but even God's grace raises eyebrows. Jesus accomplished our salvation by dying as a criminal. We may know that he was innocent of any charges, but he died shamefully nonetheless. A crucified Messiah has never been a popular image of a savior. Moreover, Christians confess that our sins were imputed to Jesus so that he bore the punishment for them in our place. There is nothing sanitized about our redemption.

Keep in mind that the incarnate Son of God, before he died, found himself on the equivalent of the threshing floor. Jesus lived in this world and went to social events. He heard crass jokes and witnessed immorality. He was even accused of being a party animal (Matt. 11:19). There is, then, something scandalous about the gospel. My point, though, is that Jesus met people where they were and befriended them. He later died for them. God used the messy situations of his life to redeem sinners.

How does this theology inform our own moral conundrums? There is relief in knowing that a God who experienced a fallen world and died to redeem it has sympathy for our moral uncertainty. We can approach this God in prayer and be honest about our confusion and weakness. We can say, "Lord, I want to do what honors you, but I don't know how." We can admit that we cannot control what other people do and that we do not know how the situation will turn out. So far as we are able, we can determine the best way to proceed, give the results over to God, and ask him to do his will. His grace, already demonstrated at the first coming of Jesus, assures us that no situation is beyond his transforming power.

Ruth 3 teaches us that God graciously redeems all sorts of situations. Yes, there was little chance that Naomi's scheme could work. There were simply too many variables that neither Naomi nor Ruth could control. But Ruth and we serve a God who controls the variables. He does so to redeem us and the situations of our lives. He seems to delight in bringing good out of the bad, the perplexing, and the hopeless.

WHAT RUTH AND BOAZ WANTED

The scene in Ruth 3 might be awkward, but Ruth was not interested in cheap thrills. Whatever her anxiety about Naomi's plan, Ruth was there for more than herself. She proposed marriage to the boss because Boaz was a kinsman-redeemer. Both Naomi and Ruth were widows without sons. As will be discussed in the next chapter, a kinsman-redeemer had the opportunity to marry his relative's widow and preserve his line. Ruth visited Boaz because of Elimelech and Mahlon. She did not want their names or property to disappear from the community.

Let us not minimize Ruth's godliness or merely suggest that Ruth remained true to the values that her Moabite parents inculcated in her.[6] Naomi had told Ruth to wait for Boaz's instructions, but Ruth seized the initiative again (cf. 1:16; 2:2). While Naomi wanted a husband for Ruth, Ruth wanted a child for Naomi. Here was the embodiment of covenantal faithfulness (*hesed*) that showed Ruth to be a true Israelite. Because of her faith in Yahweh, she acted on behalf of the less fortunate. If her first kindness was staying with Naomi, her second kindness was marrying the man who could provide the heir. Ruth married for neither love nor money but for familial well-being. In the process, God blessed her with the other two.

By way of an aside, we should note the significance of Boaz's designation of Ruth in 3:11. He referred to her as a noble woman or a woman of character. If Boaz was a man of character (2:1), then Ruth had become his equal. She had gone from being a Moabitess, a foreigner, and one less than Boaz's servant girls to "my daughter" and now a woman of character. If we come to Ruth by way of Proverbs (as in the Hebrew canon) rather than Judges (as in the Greek and English canons), Boaz's designation for Ruth recalls the closing verses of Proverbs that praise the woman of character. In essence, Boaz considered Ruth a Proverbs

31 kind of woman. Her background meant little now for she had made a good confession of faith and demonstrated what was arguably the highest act of regard for the perpetuity of God's covenant with his people: pursuing levirate marriage. If the townspeople already knew that Ruth was a "woman of noble character," all that would remain for them to say is that she was worth more than seven sons (Ruth 4:15). What praise belongs to God for what he did in this woman's life!

Boaz also continued to demonstrate *hesed*. He readily acceded to Ruth's request to perform the role of the kinsman-redeemer and marry her. Being a kinsman-redeemer, though, involved the significant cost of caring for the widow, raising the child, and later giving the deceased relative's property to the child. That Boaz was willing to absorb the cost speaks highly of his godly character. Consider these verses from the New Testament:

> Command those who are rich in this present world not to be arrogant nor to put their hope in wealth, which is so uncertain, but to put their hope in God, who richly provides us with everything for our enjoyment. Command them to do good, to be rich in good deeds, and to be generous and willing to share. In this way they will lay up treasure for themselves as a firm foundation for the coming age, so that they may take hold of the life that is truly life. (1 Tim. 6:17–19)

> Do not store up for yourselves treasures on earth, where moth and rust destroy, and where thieves break in and steal. But store up for yourselves treasures in heaven, where moth and rust do not destroy, and where thieves do not break in and steal. For where your treasure is, there your heart will be also. (Matt. 6:19–21)

Boaz was a man rich in this present world and yet was laying up treasure in heaven by being generous and willing to share. Having experienced the blessing of God, Boaz had the assurance of God's sustaining grace and was thereby free to reach out to others in God's name. Boaz, of course, had experienced redemption from an Old Testament perspective. He had experienced divine grace through the types and shadows of the law (Heb. 10:1) that attested to God's redemptive activity on behalf of his people—activity that climaxed in the person and work of Jesus Christ. In short, Boaz had received a share not just in the Promised Land but in the eternal covenant.

But how does one respond to God's redeeming grace? Ruth told Boaz that he could be the answer to his earlier prayer in Ruth 2:12. The Hebrew word translated "corner" in Ruth 3:9 and "wings" in 2:12 is the same word:

> May you be richly rewarded by the LORD, the God of Israel, under whose wings you have come to take refuge. (Ruth 2:12)

> "Who are you?" he asked.
> "I am your servant Ruth," she said. "Spread the corner of your garment over me, since you are a kinsman-redeemer." (Ruth 3:9)

The point is that Ruth was asking Boaz to be her and Naomi's protector as well as the guarantor of Mahlon and Elimelech's stake in the Promised Land. Boaz had already shown kindness to Ruth and Naomi. He continued to show it by agreeing to marry Ruth and giving more grain. The grain, of course, represented Boaz's continuing generosity and assured the women of sustenance for an even longer period.

But there is more. Boaz said that he did not want Ruth to go back to Naomi empty-handed. The Hebrew word translated "empty-handed" appeared on Naomi's lips in Ruth 1:21 when she accused Yahweh of bringing her back to Bethlehem empty. Now Boaz signaled his intention to do more than feed Ruth and Naomi for the short term. In addition to filling their stomachs, he would take steps to fill their arms with a son who would inherit Elimelech's (and Mahlon's) property and fill their hearts with lasting hope and joy. He would relieve the levels of famine/emptiness in Ruth 1. The revelation of the nearer kinsman may add suspense, but Ruth and Naomi now knew that one kinsman, either way, would come to their aid. Boaz would see to it in the morning. The grain was the proof.

Ruth 3 may be sensually charged, but Boaz demonstrated that he was a good man—not because he avoided touching Ruth but because he agreed to marry her. He would absorb loss to himself because of love for God and neighbor. Boaz was Jesus to Ruth, Naomi, and their husbands. In fact, Boaz of Bethlehem, the house of bread, foreshadowed Jesus who was born in Bethlehem and heralded by angels to shepherds in the fields outside Bethlehem. Jesus, of course, multiplied loaves of bread for hungry crowds and became the bread of life when his body was broken on the cross for the sins of believers.[7]

We who have been saved by Jesus are, like Boaz, to be Jesus to one another. In Christ we know that God has worked all things for our good. We are confident that he will accomplish his good purpose and not fail to care for us. No matter the situation, we can practice the law of God and even look out for the interests of others in the situation. We can be instruments of righteousness and agents of redemption.

Of all that could go wrong on that threshing floor and in your life, God brings about good. No, we do not always know what good can come out of the situations of our lives, but God does. He makes no mistakes. We can believe that he is up to good on our behalf. We can act in confidence that he will use vessels of clay, even us, to bring about good in someone else's life.

FOR FURTHER REFLECTION

1. How would Hollywood likely depict the scene on the threshing floor?
2. Have you ever, in effect, found yourself on the threshing floor in the middle of the night? Were you there because of someone else's action?
3. Describe the scandal of the incarnation of the Son of God. How is Jesus' experience comforting for you?
4. Why did Boaz respond as he did to Ruth's request?
5. What might the integrity of Ruth and Boaz look like for you today?

7

THE BOTTOM LINE

At this point, we should pause to look more closely at the term "kinsman-redeemer" (Heb. *go'el*) in Ruth 2:20 and 3:9. Naomi used it first with reference to Boaz after Ruth returned from her first day of gleaning in his field:

> "The Lord bless him!" Naomi said to her daughter-in-law. "He has not stopped showing his kindness to the living and the dead." She added, "That man is our close relative; he is one of our kinsman-redeemers." (Ruth 2:20)

Ruth later incorporated it into her request for marriage when she and Boaz met on the threshing floor:

> "Who are you?" he asked.
> "I am your servant Ruth," she said. "Spread the corner of your garment over me, since you are a kinsman-redeemer." (Ruth 3:9)

A full-orbed understanding of the Hebrew word *go'el* comes from seeing this term in a larger context, that is, in relation to the theological significance of the land. Together, land and kinsman-redeemer get at the bottom line of biblical religion.

THE LAND AS THE STAGE FOR MISSION

In the Old Testament, the land (or earth) always belongs to Yahweh simply because he created it. In a poetic summary of Genesis 1, Psalm 24:1–2 says,

> The earth [or land] is the LORD's, and everything in it,
>> the world, and all who live in it;
> for he founded it upon the seas
>> and established it upon the waters.

Psalm 95:5 similarly affirms,

> The sea is his, for he made it,
>> and his hands formed the dry land.

As rightful owner, Yahweh could give land to whomever he wished, whether his people or the other nations. Whereas he promised the patriarchs all the land encompassed by the dimensions in Joshua 1:4, Yahweh forbade the Israelites to dispossess certain nations, including Moab, of the territory that he had allotted for them (e.g., Deut. 2:9). Israel may have been the elect nation, but Yahweh ruled the whole world with care and beneficence for all. He gave all peoples a share in his creation:

> When the Most High gave the nations their inheri-
>> tance,
>> when he divided all mankind,
> he set up boundaries for the peoples
>> according to the number of the sons of Israel.
>>> (Deut. 32:8)

Even so, neither the Israelites nor the nations ever assumed ultimate ownership of their divinely allotted land. The flow of history and the oracles against the nations in the prophetic books teach that no human kingdom wielded power for long. Yahweh gave the kings of the earth their momentary dominion and domains and then took them away (Dan. 2:21). He held Israelite and non-Israelite magistrates accountable for whether they ruled for the good or, just as often it seemed, the hurt of others (e.g., Jer. 22:11–17; Amos 1:6–8). Their power and the land on which they wielded it never ceased to be derived.

A related truth applied to the Israelites. According to Leviticus 25:23, the Israelites were aliens and tenants on Yahweh's land. Land was a gift or, in Israel's case, a trust. As a gift, the land was not to be used only for personal advancement. Indeed, God would bless Israel's working of the land for the provision of their needs:

> For the LORD your God is bringing you into a good land—a land with streams and pools of water, with springs flowing in the valleys and hills; a land with wheat and barley, vines and fig trees, pomegranates, olive oil and honey; a land where bread will not be scarce and you will lack nothing; a land where the rocks are iron and you can dig copper out of the hills. (Deut. 8:7–9)

> The LORD will send a blessing on your barns and on everything you put your hand to. The LORD your God will bless you in the land he is giving you. (Deut. 28:8)

For this reason, provision of needs and wants was not to consume Israel's attention. Instead, the land was to be the stage for ministry, or in the words of Alicia

Ostriker "an instrument of generosity."[1] The Israelites were to use economics to address the so-called felt needs of one another and others with a view to gaining opportunities to discuss the distinct beliefs and motives of Israelite theology and ethics. It was this ministerial view of economics that would get the attention of people outside Israel and promote conversation and even conversion.

What was happening in Israel was related to the so-called creation mandate in Genesis 1:26–28:

> Then God said, "Let us make man in our image, in our likeness, and let them rule over the fish of the sea and the birds of the air, over the livestock, over all the earth, and over all the creatures that move along the ground."
>
> So God created man in his own image, in the image of God he created him; male and female he created them. God blessed them and said to them, "Be fruitful and increase in number; fill the earth and subdue it. Rule over the fish of the sea and the birds of the air and over every living creature that moves on the ground."

God had created humans in his image to rule over creation, that is, to tap and realize its potential for the glory of God. Humans were not autonomous kings but vice-regents. Their responsibility to God, however, went beyond caretaking and maintenance to development of a culture and civilization that utilized the material world for the flourishing of the arts and sciences. Humans, animals, and plants would mutually benefit from a responsible and unselfish development of the earth's raw resources. Economics or commerce was the instrument to distribute and share the richness that came from individuals' specialized mastery of the created order. But, alas, humanity quickly entertained an illusion of autonomy, renounced the Creator's mandate, and exploited the earth to the detriment of the whole creation. Evil escalated out of control twice, necessitating first a flood (Gen. 6) and then the confusion of languages (Gen. 11). The realization of the creation mandate seemed unattainable because the vice-regent would not accept his or her place before God.

Not to be frustrated, God graciously singled out Abraham and his descendants and put them on a relatively small tract of land where they, in a restored relationship with him, might begin to reverse the race's plunge into self-destruction. They would be a redeemed community that modeled commerce, justice, and compassion. This small experiment in redemption of one man and his family would be the means by which God would reconcile a fallen creation to his eternal plan. The location, Canaan, was no accident. It lay at the crossroads of civilization and strategically became the base for God's redemptive activity in the world. Described as a land flowing with milk and honey, Canaan was a down payment on paradise restored.

The descendants of Abraham were the new Adam with charge of a new Garden of Eden, but they were not to keep the garden to themselves. In Exodus 19:6 Yahweh constituted a recently redeemed people as a kingdom of priests. While the tribe of Levi served as priests to the nation to remind them of their sacred calling, the nation had a mediatorial ministry to their neighbors, even the whole world. From this people and this land, redemptive blessing would go out to all nations. What the tribes did on their land, that is, model a redeemed society, would draw the nations to Israel's God. They would come to Yahweh's temple, hear his law, and go home to implement it in all areas of life:

In the last days

the mountain of the LORD's temple will be estab-
    lished
  as chief among the mountains;
it will be raised above the hills,
  and all nations will stream to it.

Many peoples will come and say,

"Come, let us go up to the mountain of the LORD,
  to the house of the God of Jacob.
He will teach us his ways,
  so that we may walk in his paths."
The law will go out from Zion,
  the word of the LORD from Jerusalem.
He will judge between the nations
  and will settle disputes for many peoples.
They will beat their swords into plowshares
  and their spears into pruning hooks.
Nation will not take up sword against nation,
  nor will they train for war anymore. (Isa. 2:2–4)

Once drawn to Yahweh, the nations would learn that a
right relationship with him, made possible by his gracious
redemption, was the prerequisite for just and mutually
beneficial relationships among humans. The transforming effect of God's redemption of Israel would spread
throughout the nations as they had contact with this holy
and peculiar people. By virtue of a ripple effect, a day of
small beginnings would eventually bring about the realization of the creation mandate. The nations would sing
God's praise, do art and science to discover creation's
potential, buy and sell the products of their labor fairly
(i.e., practice business ethics), and thereby establish a
God-honoring, creature-helping culture.

The distinctiveness of this missional purpose of Israel in its land is seen in the Pentateuch's disavowal of a top-down approach to economics. The eighth commandment of the Ten Commandments protected private property even before Israel entered the land. Further revelation expanded a family's private property to include individual parcels of real estate that would be part of an extended family's share of the Promised Land. The law protected private property from forced and/or permanent loss. In particular, Sabbath and jubilee laws were designed to prevent generational debt that would cause less fortunate families to lose their patrimonies to opportunistic landowners or a centralized authority. According to Christopher Wright, "Early Israelite society . . . was socially decentralized and non-hierarchical. It was geared towards the social health and economic viability of the 'lowest' units, not to the wealth, privilege or power of the 'highest.'"[2] Why was this so? The presupposition behind Israel's economic system was that "God willed all Israelites to have a relatively equal opportunity to share in the richness of the land."[3] As the tribes prepared to enter Canaan, they knew that Yahweh would give them ownership of the Promised Land and that he required them to respect each other's access to the means of production. Though equal outcome was never the vision of Pentateuchal legislation, fair and mutually beneficial dealings always were. An Israelite went about making a profit while trying at the same time to do right by his or her associates and customers.

Deuteronomy 17 may speak of a king, but the surrounding legislation obviously limited his power to an extent unknown among Israel's neighbors. Israelite kings were supposed to contrast with their ancient Near Eastern counterparts by having less land and wealth and giving more attention to promoting adherence to God's covenant. Less land and wealth for the king meant more for the subjects so that they might go about presenting a distinct witness in their vocations. Prophets later excoriated public officials who used the power of their position to defraud people of their property and reduce them to serfs (e.g., 1 Kings 21:17–19; Isa. 5:8; Amos 2:6–7). Not just each tribe but also each family had a patrimony that gave it access to the means of production. The point is that everybody in a redeemed society had a share in fulfilling the creation mandate. Everybody was, in fact, a vice-regent individually using his or her labor to develop creation's potential to the glory of God. The dignity of that calling was upheld by the inviolability of private property and the deuteronomic requirement of kings to "follow carefully all the words of this law and these decrees and not consider [themselves] better than [their] brothers" (Deut. 17:19–20).

By contrast, much of the ancient Near East had a top-down approach to economics that, to modify Christopher Wright's statement, was geared to the social health and economic viability of the highest units.[4] The crown owned virtually all property and, in effect, leased it to subjects. Individuals labored in the service of the state and the state's gods, and this commitment to statism provided the raison d'etre for the average person's existence. A central administration would collect taxable goods and allegedly redistribute them for the welfare of all and the maintenance of social order. The harmony on earth was thought to reflect the gods' preservation of the cosmos as a whole.[5] Reality, however, differed from ideology. As is no less true of variations of redistributionist theory today, wealth concentrated in the hands of the royal officials at the top. Quite simply, the ancient Near Eastern economic system "provided wealth for a few at the expense of many."[6] Religious ideology thinly masked the self-promoting agenda of elitists and robbed individuals of their dignity that comes from being vice-regents in God's world.

As described in Leviticus 25, the Pentateuch's approach to economics was hardly utopian or impractical. The Old Testament writers were acquainted with life's vagaries and vicissitudes, which had their various effects on people. Though each family was guaranteed equal opportunity in the form of a patrimony, each patrimony had its own potential that was shaped by location, topography, rainfall, soil, and other factors. These variables necessitated a division of labor and a diversity of skills. Some Israelites made their living on the sea, others on the farm, and still others on the trade routes. So-called equal opportunity, then, did not guarantee equal outcome. Like the rest of humanity, the Israelites were not created with the same abilities and given the same opportunities. They all, however, lived in the same unpredictable world. Even the most skilled and industrious worker could suffer unforeseen setbacks and find himself or herself in economic distress.

Though the Israelites faced the same challenges, hardships, and reversals as anyone else, how they handled them and those beset by them would, ideally, present a marked alternative to the business-as-usual and dog-eat-dog mentality of human commerce. Recognizing that life in a fallen world holds no guarantees, Leviticus 25:25–28 speaks of several ways that the Israelites could do business distinctly and to the glory of God:

> If one of your countrymen becomes poor and sells some of his property, his nearest relative is to come and redeem what his countryman has sold. If, however, a man has no one to redeem it for him but he himself prospers and acquires sufficient means to redeem it, he is to determine the value for the years since he sold it and refund the balance to the man to whom he sold it; he can then go back to his own property. But if he does not acquire the means to repay him, what he sold will

remain in the possession of the buyer until the Year of Jubilee. It will be returned in the Jubilee, and he can then go back to his property.

What is assumed in these verses is the necessity of land for economic solvency. If an Israelite could not meet his financial obligations, he more than likely would have to sell some or all of his property and then hire himself out to work for someone else. Just as today, he would then face the seemingly insurmountable task of providing for his family's daily needs while trying to save enough to pay off the debt.

By selling his land, a poor man did not cease to be the rightful owner of the property. Leviticus 25:23 forbade permanent sale of land and transfer of ownership. Instead, a debtor would in essence rent his land by selling its usufruct or potential produce. Stated differently, he sold future harvests, and these over time paid down the debt. Not to be overlooked in the sale of future harvests was the emphasis on personal responsibility. Due to poor choices or personal incompetency, "an entire generation or more could suffer the loss of ancestral land."[7] Of course, circumstances beyond human control (e.g., bad weather or pestilence) could produce the same effect. Both types of reversal reminded the Israelites that they lived on Someone else's property and were dependent on him to fulfill his purpose for having them there.

The best option for recovering from an economically devastating turn of events was to receive assistance from a relative—brother, uncle, cousin. According to Leviticus 25:25, the closest kinsman was to buy back the right to the property's usufruct that his poverty-stricken relative had sold out of necessity. Because the Old Testament knows nothing of the modern Great Society that redistributes wealth through taxes and social programs, there was no government safety net. Extended families had to show solidarity by looking out for each other's well-being. Of course, the possibility always existed that a poor man might not have a kinsman who could come to his rescue. His relatives might be dead so that he was alone in the world, or they might not be in a position to help because of their own limited resources.

In the absence of a kinsman with means, an impoverished man had two other options. He might at some point receive a windfall and be able to buy back his land. More often than not, the acquisition of additional resources would come through inheritance. An indebted laborer might also acquire a valuable skill, hire himself out for special projects, and make surplus "cash" to speed up the reduction of the debt. In all likelihood, though, returning to one's land by inheritance or "moonlighting" would require some time to happen. Especially with the latter possibility, "once a debtor had been ruined to such an extent that he had to surrender his land and forgo his liberty, the chances of his recovering on his own must have been very slender."[8] Again, not to be overlooked in this provision to buy back harvests is the obligation of the "new owner" to sell the usufruct back to the former and rightful owner. "The original owner's right to have his ancestral land to earn his own way took precedence over the right of the second owner to maximize profits."[9] In Israel, affirming a person's place in the covenant community and promoting his or her contribution to the mission of the community took precedence over profits. The bottom line was not the bottom line.

The last option for regaining the usufruct to one's property was the Year of Jubilee. The law of jubilee reinforced God's ownership of the land and protected everybody's share. Every fifty years, all debts were cancelled and all property returned. The jubilee would wipe the slate clean and give everyone a fresh start. God allowed commerce, ability, and variables to unfold for fifty years at a time, but he would not allow the successful to hoard all resources. Instead, a restoration of land and economic potential occurred. Nobody lost his covenantal share permanently. God never favored collectivism or massive private accumulation by wealthy land barons. Each family was to have economic independence and, more importantly, a share in the larger mission to the nations. The new Eden was about redemption, not survival of the fittest or unbridled capitalism. Land was the stage on which Israel lived out its covenantal relationship. As a peculiar people, Israel was to present a distinct witness to the nations. That witness was seen largely in the way the Israelites did business. Fairness, compassion, and self-giving were the bottom line.

If the fiftieth year gave everyone a fresh start, the intervening forty-nine years gave everyone opportunities to put his or her faith into action. God has not seen fit to restore paradise all at once; rather, he sanctifies us in the crucible of daily affairs. Godly living entails taking care of others and looking out for their welfare. The jubilee would do this if nobody else did. Still, the land was the stage on which God's relation with his people played out. If their relation was properly oriented, the land was a blessing to all. A poor relation with God was reflected in vicious and rapacious commerce. Only redemption made humanitarian concerns possible, and it was the experience of redemption that set Israel apart from the nations.

THE ROLE OF THE KINSMAN-REDEEMER

Boaz as kinsman-redeemer must be understood in view of this larger context. The Hebrew word for kinsman-redeemer, *go'el*, has to do with protecting the family. It was through the family that people participated in the covenant. They would learn the covenant from their parents, as the parents verbally taught the law of God and modeled conformity to it in daily life. The family patrimony was the tangible proof of a family's share in the people of God. By working their land, each family reaped the tangible blessing of being in relationship with Yahweh and consequently could participate through commerce in the wider redemptive mission to the nations. Because there was no centralized authority during the judges period, family solidarity had to be preserved at all cost. Individual family members had to look out for each other. There was nowhere else to turn for help.

A kinsman-redeemer promoted the life and fortunes of his family. When families were threatened, the kinsman-redeemer could come to their protection. He might reclaim a field that had been sold in time of financial distress—redemption of property (Lev. 25:25). He might buy a family member out of slavery—redemption of person (Lev. 25:47–48). He might avenge the death of a murdered member of the family—redemption of blood (Num. 35:16–21). He might marry a relative's widow to care for her and have a child—a combination of the other forms of redemption (Deut. 25:5). All these steps toward family protection and solidarity would occur because the bottom line in Israel was supposed to be covenantal faithfulness. Taking care of one's dependents and promoting their full participation in the covenant community took precedence over personal wealth or ambition.[10] In a sense, the measure of true spirituality was how one treated his or her neighbor, including family members. A right relationship with Yahweh would show in caring relationships with others. The latter, now sometimes labeled mercy ministry, would create the opportunity to discuss the former with the surrounding peoples.

Boaz willingly came to the defense of Ruth, Naomi, and their deceased husbands. While we do not know what relation Boaz had with Elimelech, he was aware that Elimelech's family and property were in distress. Getting involved would cost him. Even so, showing loving-kindness trumped all personal sacrifice. As a member of the covenant community, Boaz had experienced redeeming grace. He knew that God had rescued him from sin and given him a share of the Promised Land. Because God had made promises to Boaz, Boaz could minister to others. The same is true for us.

What happens in Ruth 3 has to do with 1 Peter 1:3–5, which speaks of the believer's inheritance in Jesus Christ:

> Praise be to the God and Father of our Lord Jesus Christ! In his great mercy he has given us new birth into a living hope through the resurrection of Jesus Christ from the dead, and into an inheritance that can never perish, spoil or fade—kept in heaven for you, who through faith are shielded by God's power until the coming of the salvation that is ready to be revealed in the last time.

The kinsman-redeemer motif, of course, anticipated Jesus Christ. In Jesus God has not allowed us to suffer loss because of our sin in particular or the effects of the fall in general. He has redeemed us through the blood of his Son who has become our fellow human. Jesus absorbed the cost for our sin and by his resurrection secured an eternal inheritance for us. We who believe in him will be raised from the dead to live with him in the place that he has prepared. In short, we will inherit the earth (Matt. 5:5). Thus, we who are poor because of sin are made rich by the poverty of his incarnation (2 Cor. 8:9). The redemption of property and the securing of family in Ruth point ahead to the redemption from sin that is accomplished by Jesus Christ for Old and New Testament saints.

Boaz may have been a kinsman-redeemer, but he along with Elimelech, Mahlon, Kilion, Naomi, Ruth, and Obed died, even as all humans do. Levirate marriage might secure a patrimony in the short run, but eventually death disinherits everyone. The New Testament especially, but also the

Old Testament, looks beyond death to an incorruptible inheritance made possible by resurrection. Death does not forever separate the deceased from this world, which is the scene of God's redemptive activity. Here is where levirate marriage in Israel differed from levirate marriage in the ancient Near East. Donald A. Leggett has demonstrated how levirate marriage in the ancient Near East, especially Assyria, showed more concern for the care of the widow than for the birth of an heir to inherit the deceased husband's estate.[11] In Israel, care of the widow was combined with an interest in preserving the association of the deceased husband's name with his property. According to Deuteronomy 25:6, the first son born of a levirate union would "carry on the name of the dead brother so that his name will not be blotted out from Israel." The Hebrew word translated "blotted out" was used by Moses in Exodus 32:32 when he offered to be punished in place of those who worshiped the golden calf. The same word also appears in Genesis 6:7 and 7:4 with reference to destroying all living creatures by a flood. In other words, to be blotted out from Israel was serious. It was to be disconnected from God's people, God's land, and even God himself.

At the very least, Deuteronomy 25:6 is saying that the dead were not forgotten and, as Jeffrey H. Tigay explains, were even thought to continue living a shadowy existence in the place of departed spirits. Tigay speaks of "the importance of perpetuating the name of the deceased" among the living, but he does not elaborate on why this is important.[12] Similarly, Herbert Chanan Brichto maintains without further explanation, "The welfare of the dead is somehow connected with the continuation of his line upon his inherited property and the more sons the greater the deceased's security."[13] That word "somehow" needs specificity. In what way was the condition of a dead man linked with the continuation of his progeny on his patrimony? Brichto denies that a belief in resurrection was involved but nevertheless insists that the Israelite belief in retribution required an afterlife. Actually, the covenant promises of God also require an afterlife as well as a resurrection.

A redemptive-historical perspective reads Deuteronomy 25:6 in view of the salvific work of Jesus Christ. What God was doing with patrimonies in the Old Testament taught his people that he would reverse the curse of Genesis 3 and give them a lasting return for the faithful labor of their hands. The patrimony represented an inviolable share in God's reconciliation of a fallen creation to his eternal plan. By inheriting his father's property, the son assumed or represented the name so that each generation pushed the inheritance into the future and thus signified the continuation of God's promise to all heirs, even those who had died.

The Old Testament is, of course, known for its numerous lists of names, and the book of Ruth ends with such a list. Since Ruth ends with a genealogy, and since the New Testament genealogies, which include the Old Testament names, end with Jesus, Jesus is the fulfillment of all the inheriting in the Old Testament. All the stress on patrimonies in the Promised Land (e.g., Josh. 13–19) and maintaining the name of the deceased (e.g., Ruth 4:10) anticipates the eternal inheritance that all believers have in Jesus. In Jesus God makes good on his promise to have a people for his name and to have unimpeded communion with them in a new creation. Jesus would later say, "And this is the will of him who sent me, that I shall lose none of all that he has given me, but raise them up at the last day" (John 6:39). He also declared that the meek would inherit the earth (Matt. 5:5). Putting these two affirmations together, we can conclude that Jesus, by means of resurrection, delivers the lasting inheritance and puts an end to emergency measures such as levirate marriage. With Jesus there are no more threats to the inheritance. He secures it fully and finally.

Thus, the Teacher's perspective on inheritance in Ecclesiastes is not the normative perspective of either Testament:

"Meaningless! Meaningless!"
    says the Teacher.
"Utterly meaningless!
    Everything is meaningless.
What does man get from all his labor
    at which he toils under the sun?" (Eccl. 1:2–3)

I denied myself nothing my eyes desired;
    I refused my heart no pleasure.
My heart took delight in all my work,
    and this was the reward for all my labor.
Yet when I surveyed all that my hands had done
    and what I had toiled to achieve,
everything was meaningless, a chasing after the
        wind;
    nothing was gained under the sun. . . .

Then I thought in my heart,
"The fate of the fool will overtake me also.
    What then do I gain by being wise?"
I said in my heart,
    "This too is meaningless."
For the wise man, like the fool, will not be long
        remembered;
    in days to come both will be forgotten.
Like the fool, the wise man too must die!

So I hated life, because the work that is done under the sun was grievous to me. All of it is meaningless, a chasing after the wind. I hated all the things I had toiled for under the sun, because I must leave them to the one who comes after me. And who knows whether he will be a wise man or a fool? Yet he will have control over all the work into which I have poured my effort and skill under the sun. This too is meaningless. So my heart began to despair over all my toilsome labor under the sun. For a man may do his work with wisdom, knowledge and skill, and then he must leave all he owns to someone who has not worked for it. This too is meaningless and a great misfortune. (Eccl. 2:10–11, 15–21)

Both passages doubt and even deny a lasting return for one's labor. Death levels all achievement and strips one of an eternal inheritance.

The Teacher, however, confines his philosophizing to "under the sun." In other words, he has a naturalistic epistemology that has no recourse to revelation from beyond the sun. His teaching does not take into account the covenant of a self-revealing God with his people. The covenant name for God, Yahweh, never appears in Ecclesiastes. If, as the rest of the Bible teaches, death is the punishment for sin and God's grace is the cure, then not even death ultimately can disinherit any of God's people from the restored creation that Canaan foreshadowed. Without the resurrection of Jesus to which 1 Peter 1 refers, the promise of inheritance in both Testaments fails and the Teacher in Ecclesiastes has the last word. Because of the resurrection, all who are saved by Jesus (and there is salvation in no other name) have certainty of receiving what God has promised, whatever vagaries still beset God's people in this world that has not yet been fully delivered from the curse for sin.

GOD AS KINSMAN-REDEEMER

In the Old Testament, go'el is used more often of God than of humans. He redeemed his people from captivity to foreign oppressors, especially the Egyptians:

Therefore, say to the Israelites: "I am the LORD, and I will bring you out from under the yoke of the Egyptians. I will free you from being slaves to them, and I will redeem you with an outstretched arm and with mighty acts of judgment." (Ex. 6:6)

In your unfailing love you will lead
    the people you have redeemed.
In your strength you will guide them
    to your holy dwelling. (Ex. 15:13)

He saved them from the hand of the foe;
    from the hand of the enemy he redeemed them.
        (Ps. 106:10)

God made no payment to Pharaoh; instead, he acted as kinsman-redeemer to secure, even force, his people's liberation. As Redeemer, God has power to change circumstances and bring a world gone awry into conformity with his purpose.

With reference to the exile, Isaiah spoke of a second exodus by which God, the Redeemer, would deliver his people from the Babylonians:

This is what the LORD says—
    your Redeemer, the Holy One of Israel:
"For your sake I will send to Babylon
    and bring down as fugitives all the Babylonians,
    in the ships in which they took pride." (Isa. 43:14)

Leave Babylon,
    flee from the Babylonians!
Announce this with shouts of joy
    and proclaim it.
Send it out to the ends of the earth;
    say, "The LORD has redeemed his servant
        Jacob." (Isa. 48:20)

Burst into songs of joy together,
>   you ruins of Jerusalem,
> for the Lord has comforted his people,
>   he has redeemed Jerusalem. (Isa. 52:9)

For a time, Babylon had served as God's penal agent (Isa. 47:6), but God, Isaiah announced, would do a new work in the lives of his people. Judgment would not have the last word. The descendants of Abraham would fulfill their mission of being a light to the Gentiles. God is neither static nor dead but ever active to accomplish his plan, which no one can thwart.

What is clear in Isaiah is that God's redemption is unconditional. Israel had plainly broken God's law and brought reproach to his name. They deserved nothing more from him but wrath. Yet God did not give up on his people. Though they had sinned against him by disregarding his covenant, God graciously and sovereignly redeemed them. If kinsman-redeemers came to the defense of family members, God in the person of Jesus Christ has come to our defense and secured our deliverance from sin. Matthew 1:21 says that Jesus will save his people from their sin. Jesus has come in the likeness of sinful humanity to be a sin offering for both Jews and Gentiles. Jesus did not die to make salvation merely possible for everybody. He died for those who put their trust in him and receive by faith the redemption that he accomplished. He actually saves people from sin and obtains an eternal inheritance for them. In Christ you have a part in God's family (Rom. 8:16–17). Your inheritance is reserved in heaven (Col. 1:12, 1 Peter 1:3–4). Hence, there is a future for you.

As it turns out, redemption involved great cost to God. God did not pay a price to anyone but himself. He satisfied his own justice through the blood of his Son. Jesus paid the price or wages for our sin (cf. Rom. 6:23). Thus, God is consistently just and the one who justifies. God, who wants a people for his name, does everything necessary to create such a people. We who are a new creation in Christ become profitable servants who bear witness to God's redeeming grace (Isa. 43:6–12).

If God has gone to these lengths, we can trust him. Hebrews 9:12 speaks of the eternal redemption that Jesus' blood obtained. With that assurance God's people call upon their Redeemer in the day of trouble. They remember God's redemptive activity in the past (Ps. 74:2; 77:15) and plead for him to act redemptively again (Ps. 69:18; 119:154). If the kinsman-redeemer motif offers protection and sustenance for families ravished by life in a fallen world, Jesus as the resurrected kinsman-redeemer provides assurance that goes beyond this life into eternity (Job 19:25; Hos. 13:14; Rom. 8:34; 1 Cor. 15:55–57). Nothing in this life or the next can separate God's people from their Redeemer.

For this reason, they can act redemptively toward one another. Jesus may fulfill the kinsman-redeemer motif, but he calls his people to demonstrate a similar advocacy toward one another as he has given to us. The teaching about adoption in Romans 8, the body metaphor in 1 Corinthians 12, and all of the "one another" passages throughout the New Testament inform us who believe in Jesus that we are part of God's family, even brothers and sisters in the Lord. As a kinsman-redeemer would look out for the welfare of a disadvantaged family member, so we Christians should bear one another's burdens and care for one another's needs. We might not go so far as practicing levirate marriage, though doing so is not unknown in Africa,[14] but God still calls his people to submit themselves to each other for the good of the community of faith. What submitting to each other looks like in any given situation requires creative adaptation of the "one another" passages. Each believer's security in Christ and God's promise to provide for his people free individuals to minister to others out of the riches of God's grace.

FOR FURTHER REFLECTION

1. What does it mean that your possessions and resources are a trust from God?
2. How might you fulfill the creation mandate to tap creation's potential for the glory of God?
3. What would it look like for you personally to do business in a just, compassionate, and God-honoring way?
4. How might the Christians with whom you regularly worship more corporately model a redeemed community? How might the broader church?
5. What application might the Sabbath year and jubilee laws have for God's people today?
6. Compare Boaz as a kinsman-redeemer with Jesus as a kinsman-redeemer.

8

MEET MR. SO-AND-SO

When I preached a series of sermons on Ruth, one of the parishioners said with some disappointment that there does not seem to be much romance in the book. Instead, Naomi, Ruth, and Boaz seemed to be more concerned about survival and duty. There is a measure of truth to this observation.[1] The text does not say that Boaz was the most eligible bachelor in town who fell in love with the beautiful damsel in distress. Perhaps he was already married and had children. Maybe he was a widower. Given what he said in Ruth 3:10 about the possibility of Ruth running after younger men, Boaz was apparently older than Ruth, but how much older is impossible to know. These considerations, however, do not take away from the insight of the parishioner. The relationship of Boaz and Ruth involved more than personal attraction to each other.

Even so, I would not give up completely on the romance. The tension in Ruth 3:12 brilliantly yet agonizingly plays on the reader's expectation: "Although it is true that I am near of kin, there is a kinsman-redeemer nearer than I." Because of all that has happened so far, we want Ruth and Boaz to be together, not Ruth and the other kinsman. Moreover, how Boaz acted would indicate that he wanted to marry Ruth for more than duty. He had had nothing but praise for her and readily agreed to a marriage proposal after being awkwardly awakened in the middle of the night. Furthermore, Naomi's comment about Boaz's impatience in Ruth 3:18 arouses curiosity. Is it only because of duty that Boaz "will not rest until the matter is settled today"? Boaz very well may have been a bachelor who found true love later in life.

More importantly, though, he was an honorable man whom God used mightily. The book may do nothing more than hint at the romance between Boaz and Ruth, but it clearly trumpets covenantal faithfulness. Above all, Boaz was a man of faith and integrity. He cared about keeping God's instruction because he knew that this was the avenue for ministering to real people with real needs and so advancing God's redemptive plan through his life. Here is where the story speaks to you and me. Do we see the situations of our lives as opportunities to glorify God by ministering to others, or do we view our situations in terms of other agendas? Whose kingdom are we building? Ruth 4 asks if we love God enough to put ourselves at his disposal by loving our neighbor.

THE PROCEEDINGS AT THE GATE

Consider the nearer kinsman. Boaz waited for him at the gate and then flagged him down on his way to work in the fields. Boaz surely knew his name, but the writer referred to him as *peloni almoni*. The NIV's "my friend" is an interpretive rendition that potentially leads the reader to think inaccurately about the nearer kinsman. *Peloni almoni* means "such-and-such" or "so-and-so" (cf. 1 Sam. 21:2; 2 Kings 6:8). For our purposes, *peloni almoni* is Mr. So-and-So, an anonymous relative of Elimelech. This designation should be understood not as a friendly way to identify the nearer kinsman but as a pejorative term. To the writer of the book of Ruth, Mr. So-and-So was not an honorable man whom God remembered by name. In this situation Mr. So-and-So thought only of himself and his interests. He would gladly add Elimelech's property to his own holdings. When reminded of marriage to Ruth and raising an heir for Elimelech and Mahlon, he changed his mind in a hurry.

At this point, we have to deal with some technical matters. Ruth 4:3 says that Naomi was selling her husband's land. Naomi was not selling the land itself but the usufruct of the land, that is, its potential produce. When this happened, the landowner typically sold a certain number of harvests before the Year of Jubilee, which would then cancel all debts and return the property to its rightful owner. By virtue of age and gender, Naomi was not able to farm the land and prosper from its produce. Land was supposed to pass from one male to another, but Naomi had no living son to inherit her deceased husband's property, work it, and take care of her. She was selling the use of the land to a kinsman so that she could benefit from his purchase of the usufruct.

It is not unusual to find learned readers of Ruth disturbed by Naomi's sale of land. Land usually passed from father to son, not father to daughter or husband to wife. Numbers 27, however, indicates that women could inherit land in the event that a man died without having fathered a son.[2] If a daughter inherited land, Numbers 36 further legislates that she had to marry within her father's tribe so that the land remained in the extended family. If Numbers 27 presents an extraordinary case, the book of Ruth deals with an even more challenging turn of events. Naomi was a widow without any children. What seems apparent, though, is that she had inherited her husband's property. This in itself is not problematic. The problem is that she was beyond childbearing years and would die childless. If she sold the land, the Year of Jubilee would not be able to restore Elimelech's attachment to the land. The land would pass out of his immediate family, and his name would disappear from the covenant community. The land would then remain in the possession of the buyer even after the Year of Jubilee. Because Elimelech's name would no longer be attached to a patrimony, he would have lost his share in the Promised Land, and God's promise to be his God and the God of his children would be nullified.

One could make the argument that Elimelech should not have left Canaan and that he had now received his just deserts. Such a response, however, is theologically unsatisfying, even erroneous. A person's share in the covenant community depends on the promise of a gracious God, not the performance of sinful humans. The book of Ruth does not explicitly state that divine judgment had cut off Elimelech from God's people, or even that Elimelech had abandoned faith in Yahweh. In fact, the affirmation of divine grace in Ruth 1:6 and the coincidences that add up to providence lead the reader to expect a future for Elimelech's attachment to his share of the Promised Land.

There are two ways to understand this selling of the usufruct or use of the land.[3] First, Elimelech may have sold the usufruct more than ten years ago and then, when the money ran out, moved to Moab instead of becoming someone's slave. Now Naomi wanted to get it back but had no money or heir. The Year of Jubilee would, in theory, return it to Elimelech's heir, but he had none. Naomi wanted the kinsman to buy back the right of usufruct now and presumably marry Ruth to produce an heir for Elimelech. We should note, though, that Ruth 4:3–4 does not explicitly mention levirate marriage in connection with the sale of land.

The second possibility is that Elimelech may not have sold the usufruct ten years ago and went to Moab anyway. Even so, Naomi and Ruth could not farm the land themselves or have the assurance of a male heir without levirate marriage. Naomi wanted to sell the usufruct to a kinsman who, presumably, also would marry Ruth. That only Boaz and the nearer kinsman were present for the sale of Elimelech and Naomi's land in Ruth 4 would suggest that the land had never been sold to a third party.[4] Either way, Naomi knew that Ruth was part of the purchase. Whoever bought the usufruct must marry Elimelech's daughter-in-law so as to try to raise up an heir to inherit the land. According to LaCocque, "the inalienability of the land is linked to the perpetuation of the family line."[5] It was the heir who ultimately provided security.

The situation in the book of Ruth is more complicated than a standard opportunity to enact the law of levirate marriage. Normally, the kinsman-redeemer would marry his relative's widow to care for her and raise a son to inherit the deceased man's property. In the book of Ruth, two widows are involved. Both Elimelech and Mahlon needed a kinsman to care for their widows and raise an heir to inherit their property. So did Kilion, but his widow chose to stay in Moab. Naomi may very well have been beyond childbearing years, but she still needed food, clothing, and shelter. Ruth had these same needs as well as being the woman with whom the kinsman-redeemer could raise up an heir. Whoever agreed to marry Ruth, care for Naomi, and raise an heir for Elimelech and Mahlon would have to be a person of some means and a person who was willing to expend those means for the benefit of others. In contemporary terms the kinsman-redeemer would have to attend Little League games and pay for piano lessons, braces, and college—all the responsibilities that come with being a parent. He would also have to put an addition on the house for his new, and perhaps second, mother-in-law.

Boaz chose at first to mention the land to the nearer kinsman and say nothing about Ruth. Whatever rhetorical skill was displayed with this approach, other factors were involved. For the men gathered at the gate, issues of property rather than marriage would more appropriately fall within their power to decide. More significantly, settling the matter of the usufructuary rights to Elimelech's land was the key to answering Ruth's petition on the threshing floor—whether Boaz had a romantic interest in Ruth or not.[6] Along these lines, it should also be noted that Ruth was not being reduced to a piece of merchandise. She wanted Boaz to marry her so that together they might produce an heir to redeem her deceased father-in-law and husband's property. By going to the gate and discussing usufructuary rights with the nearer kinsman and witnesses, Boaz acted properly (i.e., covenantally) and lovingly (perhaps even romantically) on Ruth's request. Charges of uncaring patriarchy are unfairly leveled at Boaz. Law and order need not be sterile or oppressive. In this seemingly hopeless situation, law and order were the way forward to prevent scandal on the one hand and produce a happy resolution on the other.[7]

During the deliberations at the gate, Mr. So-and-So showed his true colors. If the whole town had been talking about Naomi's return and Ruth's character, it is hard to imagine that the nearer kinsman remained in the dark about these current events. When Boaz met him at the gate, he surely could deduce that acquiring Elimelech's property involved levirate marriage to Naomi or Ruth. He must have already known that Elimelech, Mahlon, and Kilion had no children and that Naomi was beyond childbearing years. When he initially agreed to buy the property, was he feigning ignorance of Ruth's accompaniment of Naomi? Or did he not think that levirate marriage could occur with a foreigner, especially a Moabitess? If he bought the land without marrying Ruth, he knew that it would become part of his holdings that he could pass on to his own children. By not marrying Ruth, he prevented an heir from being born. If he married Ruth, then a child from that union would inherit the land, and Mr. So-and-So would lose money on the deal. Mr. So-and-So comes across as a calculating businessman. His only concern appeared to be the bottom line. The thought of giving of himself for others, especially his deceased relatives, was not on his radar screen. He seemingly had no appreciation for grace, either received or given. Instead, he exercised his legal right of first refusal.

To recall one of Jesus' parables, the nearer kinsman buried his talent rather than take the risk of multiplying it (cf. Matt. 25:14–30).[8] In some sense, he resembled Orpah who acted according to conventional wisdom and so disappeared from the narrative. At least she was named. Worse than Orpah, though, the nearer kinsman used the law for his own advantage and callously left two widows in their plight and two male relatives without attachment to an inheritance in the Promised Land. Given the perpetuity of God's covenant and the Bible's affirmation of resurrection, the nearer kinsman had essentially declared his lack of belief or interest in the future hope of God's people. Unlike Boaz, he would not "maintain the name of the dead with his property" and so witness to the confidence of God's people to inherit an eternal share in the restored creation that the Promised Land foreshadowed.

It is hard not to conclude that the nearer kinsman was a worldly person storing up treasure on earth. Jesus would say that such treasure does not last. It is certainly turned over to others at the moment of death. Another way of stating this truth is that "to hold fast to our own ambitions will lead to the loss of all," including a good name.[9] In fact, the man who will not "maintain the name of the dead" has no name. "Anonymity implies judgment."[10] By contrast, time, talent, and resources invested in God's kingdom bring a lasting return and honorable mention on the last day, if not before.

In truth, the nearer kinsman exemplified the motivation behind legalism. He did no more than the law required, but his law-keeping was devoid of love. We surely cannot claim to love God and not keep his commandments; otherwise, love becomes vague and ultimately self-defined.[11] Even so, love may be no less than meticulously keeping the law, but it is far more. Love goes beyond the moral baseline of the law to self-sacrifice for the benefit of others. In addition to keeping the law so as not to harm others, love also includes seizing opportunities to promote the welfare of others, even at cost to oneself.

Intellectual honesty also requires recognizing that the law allowed a relative to pass on serving as kinsman-redeemer. Eryl W. Davies correctly observes that levirate marriage "was not clothed with any legal sanction."[12] It is conceivable that a relative might not have had the means to take responsibility for a widow and a son without also jeopardizing his provision of the basic needs of his own family. The allowance of passing on levirate marriage, however, seems to have something else in mind. It was a test of love for God primarily and one's neighbor secondarily. Love may need the defining content of divine law, but love cannot be coerced. It must well up and pour out from a heart overflowing with both unbounded gratitude for God's gracious generosity and unquenchable trust in his providential goodness. A kinsman-redeemer went beyond the law and voluntarily gave of himself for the benefit of others and ultimately for the advancement of God's covenantal purposes. It is the promotion of God's redemptive interests in a fallen world that a kinsman-redeemer desired above all other legitimate concerns and ambitions. To anticipate the teaching of Jesus, the kinsman-redeemer was willing to sell everything for the kingdom of God. Making everything available for God's service demonstrated how much he wanted what God wants. "The story of Ruth is the story of *hesed* motivating beyond the letter of the law."[13] Without this compassionate regard for others that exceeds the law's requirement, "there is no story of Ruth."[14]

All of us are tempted to think and act like Mr. So-and-So. We are back to the conventional wisdom that was mentioned in a previous chapter. We size up a situation and figure out what is best for us. We play it safe to protect our own interests and agendas. We do not seek first the kingdom of God (Matt. 6:33). Instead, we are more concerned about "all these things" that God promises to add. Such an approach to life does not honor God. It puts our interests in the situation ahead of what God's interests might be. The anonymity of Mr. So-and-So is telling. There is no future in a life devoted to self and playing it safe. Here was a man who had an opportunity to redeem a desperate situation. He thought only of himself and so has been forgotten.

By contrast, Boaz was willing to absorb personal loss in order to do what was right and good. He modeled faithfulness to the law, compassion for others, and generosity to the needy. Notice what he said in Ruth 4:10 and compare it with Ruth's words in 3:9:

> I have also acquired Ruth the Moabitess, Mahlon's widow, as my wife, in order to maintain the name of the dead with his property, so that his name will not disappear from among his family or from the town records. (Ruth 4:10)

> "I am your servant Ruth," she said. "Spread the corner of your garment over me, since you are a kinsman-redeemer." (Ruth 3:9)

If Ruth proposed marriage for the benefit of Elimelech and Mahlon, as seen in her reference to Boaz as a kinsman-redeemer, Boaz agreed to marriage for the same unselfish reason. Through him God was able to redeem an otherwise hopeless situation. Whereas Ruth was not able to bear children before (and perhaps the physiological cause lay with Mahlon), the author of the book says in Ruth 4:13

that Yahweh opened her womb. Our faithfulness becomes the stage for God to perform mighty deeds. Through us God works out his redemptive plan. It is not as if our decisions force God's hand, but he has mysteriously chosen to work in concert with human activity.

What can make Boaz or us different from Mr. So-and-So? All of us enter this world predisposed to act according to our selfish inclinations, and we might, at first glance, surmise that Boaz was acting out of self-interest here. Look at how he set up Mr. So-and-So. He got him salivating over the land and then mentioned marriage to Ruth. It would appear that Boaz was skilled at negotiating a deal and getting the girl. Neither of these strengths necessarily casts doubt on Boaz's integrity. Boaz had shown himself to be a good man, a man of character. He could have tried to ignore the nearer kinsman's claim. Instead, he showed patience, disclosed all relevant information, and gave Mr. So-and-So his rightful opportunity. Boaz accepted the possibility that he might not get either the land or, more regrettably it would seem, Ruth. Everything was done in the open with respect for the law and God's will. There was no shame in wanting to be the kinsman-redeemer and Ruth's husband. Neither desire was less pure than the other. Where Boaz showed his true colors was in following the law in order to discover what Yahweh wanted.

What made Boaz a noble person is what potentially makes you and me noble. Boaz was a man of God. He had experienced God's redeeming grace that transforms character. That grace comes through Jesus Christ who died to subdue our selfishness. Without Christ we live for ourselves and look out for ourselves. Because of Christ, we die to self and look out for Christ's interests. This is not to say that we have no interests. It seems fair to say that Boaz wanted to marry Ruth. But we, as he, must patiently and obediently subordinate our interests to God's.

THE BLESSING OF THE WITNESSES

Ruth 4:11–12 records the concurrence of the witnesses:

> Then the elders and all those at the gate said, "We are witnesses. May the LORD make the woman who is coming into your home like Rachel and Leah, who together built up the house of Israel. May you have standing in Ephrathah and be famous in Bethlehem. Through the offspring the LORD gives you by this young woman, may your family be like that of Perez, whom Tamar bore to Judah."

They realized the magnitude of Boaz's faith and action. They could see that they were witnessing a divine moment. People, even God's people, rarely act this way, especially in the dark days of the judges. But Boaz's action was different, and the townspeople sensed that God was up to something—hence, the references to Rachel and Leah, the mothers of Jacob's sons. God used them, in the particular messiness of their context, to fulfill the patriarchal promise of descendants and advance his redemptive plan. The witnesses prayed that God would do something redemptive through this union, as desperate as the circumstances had seemingly been and as unforeseeable as this marriage had been when Naomi returned to Bethlehem several weeks ago.

Let us not overlook the inclusion of Ruth with Rachel and Leah. However these sisters may have feuded and competed with each other (Gen. 29:31–30:24), they were patriarchal wives and the mothers of the Israelites. The witnesses accepted Ruth into the covenant community and wished that she too might be a mother of Israelites. If Rachel and Leah had built up the house of Israel and that house was, metaphorically speaking, in ruins during the judges period, the witnesses prayed that Ruth would build up, even restore, the house. What a prayer for a woman of Moabite descent! Ruth had become a true daughter of Abraham.

But notice the reference to Perez, Tamar, and Judah. Genesis 38 records the story, and it is admittedly more unsavory than the rivalry between Rachel and Leah. Here was an instance when levirate marriage went bad, and yet God brought good out of it. Tamar's first husband, Judah's son Er, died without fathering an heir. Tamar then married Onan, Judah's second son, to have a child for Er. Like Mr. So and So, Onan refused to help Tamar become pregnant. Onan died prematurely because of Yahweh's anger. Apparently thinking that Tamar would bring misfortune on a third husband, Judah withheld his third son, Shelah, from Tamar. Later masquerading as a prostitute, Tamar eventually lured Judah into sleeping with her, and twin boys, Perez and Zerah, came from the union. Here is one story that is not read often in church on Sunday morning!

It is common to refer to Genesis 37 and 39–50 as the Joseph story and treat Genesis 38 as an anomalous and unwanted intrusion into an otherwise self-contained narrative. This approach misses the centrality of Judah for the *toledot* section of Jacob in Genesis 37:2–50:26. The Hebrew word *toledot* serves as a structural marker in the book of Genesis and means "generations" or "account."[15] A *toledot* section typically says less about the person whose *toledot* section it is and more about his descendants. Therefore, what is said about Judah in Genesis 37:2–50:26 is as much a part of Jacob's *toledot* section as what is said about Joseph. Even as Joseph was a spoiled brat in Genesis 37 but matured as the story unfolded, so Judah was not a likable person either, but he was the de facto leader of Jacob's sons. As the story unfolds, he becomes the right kind of leader, and the Tamar incident contributes to the refining process. If we pay attention to the chronological notations in Genesis 37–50, Judah married a Canaanite woman soon after he and his brothers sold Joseph into slavery. He then pleaded for Benjamin's life in the presence of Joseph not too long after he acknowledged that Tamar was more righteous than he.

Here is how the chronology works. Joseph was seventeen when he went to Egypt (Gen. 37:2) and thirty when he became second-in-command to Pharaoh (Gen. 41:46). After seven good harvests and seven lean harvests, Joseph would have been forty-four. So, twenty-seven years had elapsed since Joseph went into Egypt. In that time Judah married and had three sons. Because marriage typically occurred early, it is reasonable to conclude that the Tamar incident occurred shortly before the second visit to Egypt when Judah offered himself to Joseph in place of Benjamin. We should note that the second visit occurred during the seven lean harvests. Joseph may have been a few years younger than forty-four, and Judah's surviving son (Shelah) may have been closer to his early twenties or late teens.

The point is that Judah, through the Tamar incident, became a changed and unselfish man. He, the natural leader of the brothers, learned servant leadership that puts others ahead of self and empathizes with the suffering of others. Before the second visit to Egypt, Judah who had lost two sons of his own guaranteed Benjamin's return. In Joseph's presence, Judah offered to bear the punishment for Benjamin's alleged theft of the silver cup. The stated reason for this act of vicarious atonement was that Judah could not bear to see the sorrow of his father at the loss of another beloved son. Because of his self-sacrifice before Joseph in Egypt, Judah who had modeled servant leadership received the blessing of kingship from Jacob. Judah embodied how Israelite kings should differ from their ancient Near Eastern counterparts.[16]

Interestingly, though, the witnesses at the gate did not pray that Boaz would become a leader like Judah. Boaz had certainly demonstrated the heart of a servant leader, and the book will end by recording his name in the royal line of David. Even so, the comparison is made between the son that Ruth would bear and Perez whom Tamar bore. Both mothers hardly seemed to be likely candidates to advance God's plan of redemption in deteriorating circumstances. Nevertheless, God used Gentile women and their children to be a blessing to Israelites and Gentiles. Not only were Gentiles blessed by their contact with Israelites, but Gentiles participated in the accomplishment of God's purpose. The witnesses were hopeful that Yahweh would be pleased again to fulfill his promises through the offspring of an Israelite man and a Gentile woman. What had just happened in their midst made them recall the past, and they could not help but wonder if God was not on the move again. After years of apostasy and its deleterious effects, they certainly hoped so.

Boaz similarly demonstrated unselfishness in a desperate situation. The witnesses noticed the similarity between Boaz and the changed Judah. Boaz displayed qualities fitting for the royal line of Israel. Moreover, a hopeless situation was taking a turn for the better. The witnesses began to expect God to do something amazing. Just how amazing is the subject of the next chapter.

FOR FURTHER REFLECTION

1. If Ruth and Boaz married for more than romance, what might their additional reasons teach modern Christians about God's purpose for marriage?
2. What might Mr. So-and-So look like today?
3. What does the book of Ruth teach about the needy and the care of the needy?
4. Why did the law of God allow the kinsman-redeemer to pass on levirate marriage? What does this allowance say to Christians today about the relationship of obedience and compassion?

5. Ruth 4 recalls some of the less savory incidents in the unfolding history of God's plan of redemption. Jesus' genealogy in Matthew 1 similarly names Tamar, Ruth, and Uriah's wife (Bathsheba). Why do you suppose that the Bible seemingly goes out of its way to present its human characters in a dysfunctional and tarnished way?

9

A GLORIOUS PROVIDENCE

The book of Ruth ends with a bang. Someone, though, might question my sanity at this point. After all, chapter 4 begins with a strange sandal-removing custom and ends with a list of names. The Old Testament contains many lists of names, most of them longer than this one. When reading the Bible, we tend to skip such lists or consider them scriptural Sominex. Nevertheless, I stick by my claim. This book ends with the sopranos singing at the top of their lungs. What are they singing about? They are singing about how our lives contribute to something bigger than ourselves. Hence, this chapter is entitled "A Glorious Providence." God uses our seemingly mundane lives to build the kingdom of his Son.

Much of what we have been discussing is mundane: harvesting, land inheritance, and care of widows. The book of Ruth does not feature any miracles—whether suspensions of natural law or angelic appearances to humans. There are no references to public worship or priestly ministration. No prophet thunders against the sins of God's people, calls for repentance, threatens exile, or promises restoration. Except for mentioning the judges at the beginning and King David at the end, the book has a small-town, off-the-beaten-path feel. The characters were not the movers and shakers of the ancient Near East. The events narrated would not have made the front page of the newspaper. Boaz may have been a respected and well-to-do man in Bethlehem, but Bethlehem was hardly the power center of the tribes of Israel. Micah would later identify it as "small among the clans of Judah" (Mic. 5:2). Without intending to be derogatory, we might say that Boaz was a big fish in a small pond. Moreover, the Moabites were never a superpower in the ancient Near East. What happens in this book does not seem, at first glance, to constitute a decisive irruption, or breaking in, of God into history.

At the same time, the book does not tell a secular tale. The name of God was often on the lips of the main characters. They affirmed their belief that God had influence over their lives, however ordinary and troubled those lives may have been. That said, Ruth 4:13–22 contains some stunning, big-picture information that puts the events squarely in the middle of God's plan of redemption. Ordinary lives became the scene of extraordinary turns of events. Ruth's "good fortune" of unknowingly entering Boaz's field began to renew Naomi's faith in Yahweh, and what happens in the book's final section removes any remaining doubt that he has continued to care for her. She experienced the fullness of divine blessing.

THE BIRTH OF THE HEIR

The section opens with a brief, almost formulaic, record of Ruth's marriage to Boaz and the birth of their first child. That Yahweh is said in 4:13 to grant conception might seem to be an obvious and unnecessary affirmation, except that Ruth and Mahlon were unable to have children during ten years of marriage. While the text stops short of saying that Yahweh had closed Ruth's womb (cf. 1 Sam. 1:5), the explicit attribution of the conception to Yahweh stands out in this book. Elsewhere, only in Ruth 1:6 does the author assign an event to Yahweh's activity. Both references attest to the intervention of God's favor without which the blessings of harvest and birth would not, presumably, have come. From a biblical perspective, God rules over history and nature to work out his will. Nothing happens by blind chance or human effort alone.

It is hard not to read Ruth 4:13 without recalling some other "miracle" births in the Bible. A pattern of barrenness runs throughout the early books of the Old Testament and reappears with Elizabeth in Luke 1. Beginning with Abram's wife, Sarai, Yahweh seemed to delight in delaying the fulfillment of his promise to be the God of his people and their children. When all hope for conception and delivery seemed unfounded, God blessed the wombs of certain wives and advanced his redemptive plan through their special babies. It should be understood that the mothers by themselves were not unusual people, except for their lamentable inability to become pregnant.[1] Rather, God sovereignly withheld conception for a time so that when birth eventually occurred it was traceable to his power. The reference to a woman's barrenness usually signals that God is about to perform an unexpected wonder on behalf of his people.

The women of Bethlehem, who had earlier met a defeated and discouraged Naomi at her return from Moab, could not contain their praise at the birth of Ruth's first child. What had transpired over the last year or so had convinced them that God was yet active among his people. The apostate days of the judges had not marked the end of Israel's place in the redemptive program of Yahweh. The women prayed that the son born to Ruth and Boaz would "have his name called in Israel." This expression could mean, as the NIV translates it, "to become famous." The women surely wanted the report of Obed's unlikely birth to be told throughout Israel as a witness to what Yahweh was yet doing. The dreary days of the judges did not extinguish the hope of God's people. God always has a remnant of devout and faithful believers who persevere no matter what and "love to tell the story"—God's story.

The expression "to have a name called" could also relate more directly to the book's concern for progeny. Herbert Chanan Brichto suggests that "name" in this context has the sense of "family line." Thus, "to have the name called in Israel" is another way of talking about "establishing the name of the dead on his inheritance," which is the expression that Boaz had used at the gate (Ruth 4:5).[2] Perpetuating a family line and becoming famous are not mutually exclusive translation options. Everyone who spoke in this scene—Boaz, the men who bless him, and the women who bless Obed—hoped that the union of Boaz and Ruth would put an end to the tragic cause of Naomi's grief and thus provide all Israel with a reason to celebrate the continuation of God's promise to grant an inheritance to his faithful people.

NOT JUST ANY HEIR

Still, the women could have never anticipated how Yahweh would answer their prayer. The heir of Elimelech's land turned out to be the grandfather of King David. This means that Boaz and Ruth were the great-grandparents of David. They were in the royal line, even the messianic line (Matt. 1:5). What an honor! Now Ruth and Boaz had no way of knowing any of this, and neither did the women. As far as any of them were concerned, Ruth and Boaz were average folk trying to do God's will where he had sovereignly put them. They acted faithfully because of love for God that showed itself through love for God's people. There was no ulterior motive or give-to-get strategy. Ruth and Boaz were not trying to merit favor from God. They simply evidenced their commitment to God by putting his

Word into practice. What God would do with their faithfulness was up to him. The reference to King David indicates that God was working behind the scenes to accomplish something bigger than redeeming Elimelech's land. He used their faithfulness to bring King David and, later, King David's greater son, Jesus Christ, into the world. By their faithfulness, they participated in the establishing of God's kingdom on earth and the realizing of God's plan of salvation.[3]

The same is true for you. The situations of our lives can seem mundane. We live during an era that is not much different from the period of the judges, and 1 Corinthians 1:26–27 indicates that not many of God's people in any era are movers and shakers:

> Brothers, think of what you were when you were called. Not many of you were wise by human standards; not many were influential; not many were of noble birth. But God chose the foolish things of the world to shame the wise; God chose the weak things of the world to shame the strong.

God often prefers not to make a big splash on history's stage, but he works nonetheless. And he gets the glory when extraordinary outcomes occur in the lives of ordinary, yet faithful people. In Christ God has redeemed us from the penalty and vanity of sin. We who were spiritually empty are now filled with God's Spirit. We are heirs of Christ's kingdom and of an eternal inheritance that never perishes. Even now, God is at work in our lives to build Christ's kingdom. This means that the most seemingly mundane situation is a sacred moment—an opportunity to contribute to the unfolding of God's redemptive plan. God uses our faithfulness in daily responsibilities and ministry opportunities to accomplish more than we typically realize. We do not have to possess full understanding of what

God is doing through us, nor could we. Instead, we like Ruth and Boaz must have minds and bodies yielded to our redeeming God. As we trust him to multiply the results of our service, God seemingly works behind the scenes, one set of circumstances at a time, to "put everything under [Jesus'] feet" (Heb. 2:8).

To reinforce this point, notice the name of Ruth's child: Obed. Obed means "servant" in Hebrew. Naomi's grandson, who by levirate marriage was also reckoned to her as a son, would serve her, Elimelech, Mahlon, and Ruth by maintaining Elimelech and Mahlon's attachment to their patrimony and caring for Naomi and Ruth in their advancing years. Boaz would appreciably have a hand in this, but Obed embodied the assurance of God's faithfulness to keep his promises and give his people an inheritance.

"Servant" is a rich term in the Bible, especially in Isaiah, Zechariah, and Job. If the barrenness of Ruth reminds us of other childless women through whom Yahweh advanced his plan of redemption, the word "servant" is just as theologically laden. It is hard not to read about Obed in view of other servants.

The book of Isaiah, of course, is known for its servant songs, the fourth of which is found in chapter 53. John N. Oswalt has helpfully understood the overarching theme of Isaiah to be servanthood.[4] Before the book of Isaiah reaches its climax with a suffering servant in chapter 53, it wrestles with the reality of Israel as an unprofitable servant. As God's servant, Israel was supposed to be a channel of redemptive blessing to the nations. The nations would come to God's temple, hear the law of God, and be changed by it. In this regard, Israel as God's servant and Israel as a kingdom of priests are complementary themes. Too often, though, Israel wanted to imitate the nations and play the ancient Near Eastern game of power politics. She was anything but a profitable servant that presented a distinct witness. Consequently, she rarely was a blessing to others. To capture the futility of Israel's mission, Isaiah used the metaphor of a pregnant woman that gives birth to wind. Perhaps worse than not getting pregnant is having a pregnancy end without the birth of a healthy child. Isaiah pointedly said, "We have not brought salvation to the earth; we have not given birth to people of the world" (Isa. 26:18). But giving birth to salvation was the servant's mission.

How, then, would an unprofitable servant become a profitable servant and accomplish its mission? Isaiah 6 introduces the solution. Even as Isaiah was cleansed by the hot coal from the altar and became a prophet, so Isaiah's people, God's servant, would be cleansed by another, but closely related, servant who would suffer for sinners by offering himself as an atoning sacrifice. An unprofitable servant becomes a profitable servant through the intercession of a suffering servant. It is not by accident that Isaiah 54 and 55, which speak of mission to the nations and the free offer of the gospel, follow Isaiah 53.

Two hundred years after Isaiah, Zechariah expanded Isaiah's servant theme. In Zechariah 3:8–9, Joshua the high priest is said to be symbolic of God's servant, the Branch:

> "Listen, O high priest Joshua and your associates seated before you, who are men symbolic of things to come: I am going to bring my servant, the Branch. See, the stone I have set in front of Joshua! There are seven eyes [or facets] on that one stone, and I will engrave an inscription on it," says the LORD Almighty, "and I will remove the sin of this land in a single day."

"Branch" also appears as a messianic title in Isaiah 4:2, and it is hard not to relate the branch to the shoot of Jesse in Isaiah 11:1. In other words, the term "servant" could be used of kings as well as priests. Indeed, Yahweh refers to Obed's grandson as "my servant David" (e.g., 2 Sam.

7:5). By means of the servant's priestly ministry, Zechariah said (similar to Isaiah 53) that atonement for sin would occur in one day. If, as Exodus 28:9–12 and 21 report, the high priest's ephod and breastpiece had stones engraved with the names of the tribes (two stones with six names each on the shoulders and twelve stones with one name each on the chest), Zechariah saw one stone on Joshua the high priest, and the seven facets were engraved with the totality of God's people whose sin would be removed in a single event by the priestly ministry of the Servant/Branch. Moreover, Zechariah daringly said in 6:12–13 that the offices of king and priest would converge on the Branch, who according to chapter 3 is also the servant. Zechariah went on to describe how a shepherd (or a king) would be rejected and smitten by an unfaithful people, resulting in the opening of a fountain that would cleanse from sin (Zech. 11:8; 12:10; 13:1). The point to be made now is that the servant theme encompasses a large amount of material in the Old Testament and draws related concepts together in order to explain how God redeems a people for his name. The meaning of the name Obed links the book of Ruth with this large theme of servanthood that has to do with the provision of atonement for Jews and Gentiles.

Job should also factor into a discussion of the servant theme. Job is identified as a servant at the beginning (1:8) and end (42:8) of the book. In both contexts Job interceded for people—first his children and then his three friends. Between the references to Job as a servant, Job experienced tremendous physical and mental suffering—not unlike Naomi. Whatever else can be said about Job the man, he was a righteous and suffering servant who interceded for others. Somehow the suffering for which Job received no explanation was related to his intercessory ministry. God brought blessing to others out of the trials of one of his dear saints.

The New Testament, of course, identifies Jesus Christ as Isaiah's suffering servant (Matt. 12:17–21; Acts 8:32–35) and Zechariah's smitten shepherd (Matt. 26:31; 27:9–10). Job also foreshadows Jesus the righteous sufferer, who continually makes intercession for those who believe in him. On Jesus converge the offices of priest and king. Through his holding of these offices, Jesus saves his people from their sin and secures an eternal inheritance for them. Themes introduced in the Old Testament find their definitive realization in God's incarnate Son as well as those who believe in him. Paul, James, Peter, John, and Jude identified themselves as servants of God. In Acts 13:47, Paul and Barnabas read Isaiah 49:6, part of the second of the so-called servant songs of Isaiah, with reference to their first missionary journey among Gentiles.

All of these references indicate that a servant is used of God to advance his purposes in his world. It is proper and necessary to view Obed against this larger context. He may not be *the* servant, that is, God's incarnate Son, but he is one of many servants that showcase God's faithfulness to his announced plan to reconcile a fallen world to his eternal purpose and have a people for his name. Obed was not just a miracle child for Naomi and Ruth. Yes, he would inherit Elimelech's property and preserve his name. Even more stunning, though, is his place in the messianic line. Through him, God's plan of redemption continued to unfold in amazing fashion. As grandfather of David, he was an ancestor of Jesus and of us who believe in Jesus. God used and uses Obed, David, Jesus, and us as servants to do his will. We reign with Christ, the servant of servants, and contribute to the accomplishment of God's kingdom purpose and worldwide mission.

It is not unusual for scholars to consider the genealogy a later addition that modifies the original purpose for the book. Without the genealogy, the book supposedly reaches a satisfactory conclusion with Obed in the arms of Naomi.

To some extent, this observation is true. If the book moves from empty stomachs and arms to full stomachs and arms, the genealogy is not required to demonstrate how Naomi's initial assessment of Yahweh's involvement in her circumstances was mistaken. Even though Naomi returned without food or sons, Yahweh's ultimate purpose was not to witness against her but to show his grace through the provision of levirate marriage. We should not miss that the book of Ruth teaches this much—with or without the genealogy.

Nevertheless, we should also recognize that the book says more, and the genealogy is the major clue to the larger message of the book. Here is where some recent writers have partially missed the purpose for the book of Ruth. Feminist writers have emphasized the bond of friendship between Naomi and Ruth—a relationship that supposedly steeled two women to assert their independence in a man's world and provide for themselves. The book would seem to counter this interpretation of its data by ending with the marriage of Ruth and Boaz, the birth of Obed, and the rejoicing of the townspeople—all traditional happenings. That Ruth married Boaz cannot be denied and so must otherwise be considered an unfortunate, if not inevitable, capitulation to patriarchy.[5] Still, the message of Ruth purportedly celebrates self-reliance, self-respect, independence, and winning the respect of others.[6] In a word, then, Ruth is about power, especially the seizure of power by the underdog. For this approach to the book of Ruth, the Davidic genealogy at the end of chapter 4 is not a positive development. Rather, it along with the reference to the judges in chapter 1 provides the negative framework in which the laudable self-assertion of Naomi and Ruth occurred.[7]

Is Ruth obsessed with power, or are the recent writers? Have they read their agenda into a book whose plain sense, especially in the context of the rest of the Bible, is just the opposite? The Bible promotes humility, dependence, trust, sacrifice, and faithfulness. All of these unnatural virtues are made possible by being in relationship with a covenant God, even Jesus Christ who gave up his life for the redemption of others. In their respective ways, Ruth and Boaz, because of their relationship with this covenant God, exemplified self-abnegation, or what Paul calls "being crucified with Christ" (Gal. 2:20). To be crucified with Christ, however, is to be raised with him and to reign with him. In other words, God blesses the humble, unselfish, and often unheralded faithfulness of his people to the furtherance of his will and honor.

In the book of Proverbs, the wise person does not run ahead of God and press his or her self-promoting agenda. Rather, he or she waits on God, agreeing that "humility comes before honor" (Prov. 15:33). What this means practically is that God is not as interested as we tend to be in achieving the external fruits of success: position, wealth, and prestige. Instead, God is interested in character development, which is a slow and often painful process. In Ruth and Boaz, we observe the self-denying effects of two people who loved God and their neighbor. One can only wonder what Naomi, Ruth, and Boaz would say if they could read postmodern, deconstructionist, and feminist interpretations of their story. Surely they would not consider Ruth's marriage to Boaz a necessary evil. If those who espouse feminist readings of Ruth have loving and sacrificial relationships with other people, why could not Naomi, Ruth, and Boaz also have a positive evaluation of the death to self that biblical marriage and friendship require? This is not to say that justice is not important. It is to say that the book of Ruth goes beyond the desired result of justice to the root cause, namely, unselfishness, faithfulness, compassion, and servanthood. These qualities are often used of God to accomplish results bigger than oneself.

If the genealogy is a clue to the message of Ruth, so also is the name of the book. The book is named after Ruth, not Naomi. The story is not ultimately Naomi's story. While she may figure prominently in the story, the book wants to talk about something bigger than Naomi's fullness of blessing. That something bigger is how God uses the faithfulness of godly people in everyday settings to build his kingdom in all its fullness. There is the challenge to modern readers of the book. Do we believe that God will take care of us who are in Christ as he did Ruth? Our situation may or may not be as desperate as hers, but do we see it as an opportunity to glorify God by doing his will and leaving the results to him? Is his promise to provide for our needs so convincing to us that we will give ourselves unreservedly to serving him? Will we risk everything, knowing that the person who loses his or her life for Jesus' sake will find it?

FOR FURTHER REFLECTION

1. Ruth 4:13 says that God enabled Ruth to conceive, thus implying that God had not enabled her to conceive with Mahlon. What is your reaction to the sovereignty of God as the book of Ruth presents it?
2. Ruth 4:17 indicates that the women of Bethlehem named Ruth's child Obed. What does their choice of name say about their understanding of recent events? Can you describe a time in your life when an observer provided an accurate perspective on what God seemed to be doing?
3. How would the birth of Obed increase Naomi's faith? Do you think that God intentionally brings hardship into people's lives so that he might impress them with his greatness and goodness?
4. Can you describe a time in your life when a situation went from bad to worse and then to an amazing resolution that only God could have effected?

5. The birth of Obed seems nearly miraculous in the book of Ruth, and yet what is more natural than the birth of a baby? How do you see the hand of God at work in the mundane affairs of your life? What does God's ordinary providence suggest about the look of your faithfulness?

POSTSCRIPT

What reader is not moved by the final scene in the book? Naomi back home in Bethlehem (the house of bread) has enough food to eat and holds in her arms a biological grandson who is also her legal son.[1] She who accused Yahweh of bringing her back empty now enjoys life to the full. While Yahweh had never abandoned Naomi, he may have resorted for a time to a frowning providence—the inclusion of physical, intellectual, and/or emotional hardship in the will of God for his people—in order to draw her and others closer to himself. There may not be an explanation for the deaths of Naomi's husband and sons—anymore than Job learned the reason for the deaths of his children and servants—but the birth of Obed assured Naomi that God orders life's vicissitudes for the eventual and ultimate good of his people.

In the face of such an incomprehensible yet faithful God, how should humans respond? The book of Ruth contrasts the responses of Naomi on the one hand and Ruth and Boaz on the other. While all three individuals lived during the spiritual and moral chaos of the judges period, they did not always react similarly to their less than ideal circumstances. Even so, the faithfulness of Ruth and Boaz favorably impacted Naomi and appeared to have restored her confidence in God. God worked through the faithfulness of Ruth and Boaz not only to maintain Elimelech and Mahlon's attachment to their patrimony but also to bring Naomi to a deeper understanding of his care for her. Ruth's loyalty to Naomi was the primary vehicle for this spiritual lesson.

When Ruth stayed with Naomi and set foot on Boaz's property, neither woman had any way of knowing what the future would bring. They were going one day at a time. What Ruth exemplified and what Naomi learned is that trusting God's providence means believing that God will use a string of seemingly unrelated events to accomplish his good purpose. We, of necessity, make decisions that seem prudent at the time, but we are completely unaware of how those decisions will play out. While we might have dreamy hopes or calculated expectations, we cannot control the numerous and often unforeseen variables. It is trust in God's promises that enables God's people to remain constant in their faithfulness to the biblical worldview and its countercultural demands.

Readers of Ruth see that constancy in the prayers or prayerlike language that occurs throughout the book. Ronald M. Hals observed that God's name most often appears in Ruth in the prayers of the characters.[2] If the major message of the book is that God blesses the faithfulness of his people in the mundane affairs of life, a subordinate teaching is that a faithful people will commit the situations of their lives to God in prayer. Out of their private prayers that look to God to care for them will come intercessory prayer and active care for others. God's providence and his people's prayers are inextricably combined in the book of Ruth. Yes, the days of the judges were bleak, but God's people may always call on a God who transcends the worst of times and delights in bringing good out of bad. What is more, he works through the faithfulness of his humble people to do more than they could ask or imagine.

Even so, anyone who spends time with the book of Ruth cannot help but wonder if the plot is not too Pollyannaish. Our hearts may warm to the favorable outcome for Naomi and Ruth, who with Boaz and the townspeople seemingly lived happily ever after, but life's dilemmas do not always turn out so favorably. One might even say that they rarely do. And, of course, little Obed could not fill the void left in Naomi and Ruth by the deaths of Elimelech, Mahlon, and Kilion. One would even think that Orpah would be missed. While it is true that the book of Ruth, by alluding to the dark days of the judges and the unseemly relationship of Judah and Tamar, does not hide the so-called real world from its readers, the author did not have the pessimistic or cynical outlook on life in the real world that someone such as Qohelet in the book of Ecclesiastes had.[3] Whereas Qohelet concluded that life was random and meaningless, the author of Ruth emphasized the providence of God in the lives of faithful, but ordinary, people in the movement of redemptive history. This history reaches a climax first in the kingship of David and second in the reign of Jesus. In short, the book of Ruth optimistically teaches that God's people have a future.

Katharine Sakenfeld, as a result of traveling in the Far East, has observed in several writings how destitute women are bought and sold for the one commodity that, sadly, some of the world exclusively values in them, namely, their sexuality.[4] For these modern Ruths, there is no escape from poverty, exploitation, and dehumanization. There is no Boaz who responds to the grace of God in his life by rising above prejudice, showing kindness to another, and restoring dignity. There is only the never-ending nightmare of nightclubs and the like. How, then, do we take Ruth seriously and not reduce biblical religion to a fairy tale?

The reference to the judges in the opening verse would suggest that the book of Ruth, like the rest of the Bible, is aware of evil in all of its cosmic and human fullness. If the rest of the Bible does not minimize rebellion against God and its deleterious effects, then the book of Ruth, according to the principles of sound hermeneutics, must not be read without taking into account the theological message of its canonical context. The period of the judges may have been among the worst of times in Old Testament history, but it was by no means an anomaly. Amos, Hosea, and Micah, for example, could describe the degrading and injurious results of covenantal unfaithfulness during the divided monarchy. These years were just as spiritually, morally, and socially chaotic as the judges period. And the postexilic literature only mentions more of the same. The exile had not changed the heart or the conduct of God's people.

The Bible does not try to hide the ugliness of sin or wave a magic wand to dispense with it. There is no quick fix, only the sinless life of the incarnate Son of God who excruciatingly lay down his life as an atoning sacrifice for the sins of his people. By recalling how God redeemed the Judah and Tamar debacle and by linking Boaz with both Judah and David, the book of Ruth signals that it wants to be read as a chapter in the story of God's plan of redemption. That story, of course, begins with the fall of humanity into sin and the resulting chaos and misery. The story ends with the second coming of Jesus and a new earth devoid of sin, curse, suffering, and tears. In between, the story tells of the first coming of Jesus and the Holy Spirit's application of Jesus' redemptive work to the lives of believers. The point is that God has not chosen to restore a fallen, chaotic creation all at once. Rather, he is using the faithfulness of believers, day in and day out, to effect a gradual but inexorable reconciliation of all things to his eternal plan. In any generation God has his remnant that perseveres in faithfulness to the revealed Word and so contributes to the realization of the fullness of God's kingdom.

NOTES

PREFACE

1   William J. Bennett, ed., *The Book of Virtues: A Treasury of Great Moral Stories* (New York: Simon & Schuster, 1993), 296.

2   Ronald M. Hals, *The Theology of the Book of Ruth* (Philadelphia: Fortress Press, 1969), 1–2.

3   See, for example, Katharine Doob Sakenfeld, "The Story of Ruth: Economic Survival," in *Realia Dei: Essays in Archaeology and Biblical Interpretation in Honor of Edward H. Campbell, Jr. at His Retirement*, ed. Prescott H. Williams and Theodore Hiebert (Atlanta: Scholars Press, 1999), 215–27; Ursula Silber, "Ruth and Naomi: Two Biblical Figures Revived among Rural Women in Germany," in *Ruth and Esther*, A Feminist Companion to the Bible, second series, ed. Athalya Brenner (Sheffield: Sheffield Academic Press, 1999), 107; Phyllis Trible, *God and the Rhetoric of Sexuality*, Overtures to Biblical Theology (Philadelphia: Fortress Press, 1978), 166–96; Johanna W. H. van Wijk-Bos, *Ruth and Esther: Women in Alien Lands* (Nashville: Abingdon Press, 2001), 7–63.

4   For more on the redemptive-historical function of biblical characters, see Sidney Greidanus, "Redemptive History and Preaching," *Pro Rege* 19 (1990): 9–18.

5   For more on the inadequacy of moralistic sermons, see Bryan Chapell, *Christ-Centered Preaching: Redeeming the Expository Sermon*, 2nd ed. (Grand Rapids: Baker, 2005), 288–95.

CHAPTER ONE: IT WAS NOT THE BEST OF TIMES

1   Chronological notations for the patriarchs, exodus, and conquest have generated vigorous discussion among scholars. For a more "maximalist" approach to the historicity of Genesis–Joshua, see Iain Provan, V. Philips Long, and Tremper Longman III, *A Biblical*

History of Israel (Louisville: Westminster John Knox Press, 2003), 111–92.

2 Dale Ralph Davis, *Such a Great Salvation: Expositions of the Book of Judges*, Expositor's Guide to the Historical Books (Grand Rapids: Baker, 1990), 29.

3 Ibid., 51.

4 Cf. Joshua 15:63, which makes Judah, not Benjamin, responsible for the continuing Jebusite presence in Jerusalem.

5 Marc Zvi Brettler, *The Book of Judges*, Old Testament Readings (London: Routledge, 2002), 89.

6 For more on postmodernism, see Kevin J. Vanhoozer, *Is There a Meaning in This Text? The Bible, the Reader, and the Morality of Literary Knowledge* (Grand Rapids: Zondervan, 1998).

7 See Raymond B. Dillard and Tremper Longman III, *An Introduction to the Old Testament* (Grand Rapids: Zondervan, 1994), 146.

8 Cornelius Plantinga Jr., *Not the Way It's Supposed to Be: A Breviary of Sin* (Grand Rapids: Eerdmans, 1995), 7–27.

9 Daniel I. Block, *Judges, Ruth*, NAC 6 (Nashville: Broadman & Holman, 2002), 58, 72.

CHAPTER TWO: DEVASTATING GRIEF

1 Reg Grant, "Literary Structure in the Book of Ruth," *BSac* 148 (1991): 427.

2 D. R. G. Beattie, trans., *The Targum of Ruth*, Aramaic Bible 19 (Collegeville, MN: Liturgical Press, 1994), 18.

3 It can be argued, of course, that Abraham's journey to Egypt in Genesis 12 signaled weak faith in the promises of God made earlier in the chapter.

4 Mira Morgenstern, "Ruth and the Sense of the Self: Midrash and Difference," *Judaism* 48 (1999): 133.

5 Van Wijk-Bos, *Ruth and Esther*, 23.

6 Beattie, *The Targum of Ruth*, 19.

7 Katharine Doob Sakenfeld, *Ruth*, Interpretation (Louisville: Westminster John Knox Press, 1999), 24.

8 Danna Nolan Fewell and David M. Gunn, "'A Son Born to Naomi': Literary Allusions and Interpretation in the Book of Ruth," *JSOT* 40 (1988): 104.

9   A. D. Freedman, "Naomi's Experience of God and Its Treatment in the Book of Ruth," *Proceedings of the Eastern Great Lakes and Midwest Biblical Society* 23 (2003): 29; Trible, *God and the Rhetoric of Sexuality*, 169.

10 The NIV, along with the Septuagint and the Tanakh translation of the Jewish Publication Society, has understood the Hebrew verb to mean "to afflict" or "to abase" rather than "to witness against." Both the NIV and the Tanakh translation make the reader aware of the second possibility in a textual note. A discussion of the issue lies beyond the purpose of this book, though the grammatical construction favors the juridical option. See Robert L. Hubbard Jr., *The Book of Ruth*, NICOT (Grand Rapids: Eerdmans, 1988), 126, footnote 31. Even so, either translation fits Naomi's complaint. Either Yahweh had afflicted/abased Naomi by inexplicably bringing evil (i.e., misfortune) on her, or Yahweh had witnessed against her and consequently brought evil (i.e., punishment) on her. The Old Testament features complaints for both reasons, and it is hard to decide which is the case here. If Naomi thought that Yahweh testified against her, the author of the book did not necessarily share this explanation of her suffering.

11 Grant, "Literary Structure in the Book of Ruth," 432.

12 Paul David Tripp, *Suffering: Eternity Makes a Difference*, Resources for Changing Lives (Phillipsburg, NJ: P&R Publishing, 2001), 4.

13 According to Kristen Moen Saxegaard, Naomi "never falls so far [or is] so totally abandoned and tried as he [Job]. The reason for this [is] that although Naomi loses her husband, sons, land, and dignity, she always has Ruth." See her "'More Than Seven Sons': Ruth as Example of the Good Son," *Scandinavian Journal of Old Testament* 15 (2001): 264.

14 André LaCocque, *Ruth: A Continental Commentary* (Minneapolis: Fortress Press, 2004), 35.

CHAPTER THREE: BEYOND WHAT WOULD BE EXPECTED

1   Adele Berlin, "Ruth: Big Theme, Little Book," *Bible Review* 12 (August 1996): 48. Berlin's observations should be read in view of Anthony Leahy's section on assimilation in "Ethnic Diversity in

Ancient Egypt," *Civilizations of the Ancient Near East*, ed. Jack M. Sasson (Peabody, MA: Hendrickson, 2000), 232–33.

2 John Bright, *A History of Israel*, 3rd ed. (Philadelphia: Westminster Press, 1981), 149–50.

3 James C. Howell, "Ruth 1:1–18," *Int* 51 (1997): 283. Cf. Cynthia Ozick, "Ruth," in *A Feminist Companion to Ruth*, ed. Athalya Brenner (Sheffield: Sheffield Academic Press, 1993), 204–05; Bonnie Honig, "Ruth, the Model Emigrée: Mourning and the Symbolic Politics of Immigration," in *Ruth and Esther*, A Feminist Companion to the Bible, second series, ed. Athalya Brenner (Sheffield: Sheffield Academic Press, 1999), 59.

4 Beattie, *The Targum of Ruth*, 20.

5 Grant, "Literary Structure in the Book of Ruth," 439.

6 Honig, "Ruth, the Model Emigrée," 56–57.

7 Ibid., 57.

8 Laura E. Donaldson, "The Sign of Orpah: Reading Ruth through Native Eyes," *Ruth and Esther*, A Feminist Companion to the Bible, second series, ed. Athalya Brenner (Sheffield: Sheffield Academic Press, 1999), 143.

9 D. F. Rauber, "Literary Values in the Bible: The Book of Ruth," *JBL* 89 (1970): 29.

CHAPTER FOUR: HOLY RISKS

1 Greg A. King, "Ruth 2:1–13," *Int* 52 (1998): 182.

2 The term "covenantal thermometer" is taken from Christopher J. H. Wright, *Old Testament Ethics for the People of God* (Downers Grove, IL: InterVarsity Press, 2004), 77.

3 Ibid., 58.

4 Ruth 2:7 presents a translational and interpretive crux. For a discussion of the possible understandings, see Block, *Judges, Ruth*, 656–58.

5 LaCocque, *Ruth*, 63.

6 Hals, *The Theology of the Book of Ruth*, 11–12; Sakenfeld, *Ruth*, 47.

7 Jon L. Berquist, "Role Differentiation in the Book of Ruth," *JSOT* 57 (1993): 28–29. Cf. Linda Day, "Power, Otherness, and Gender in Biblical Short Stories," *HBT* 20 (1998): 111.

8 Athalya Brenner, "Naomi and Ruth: Further Reflections," in *A Feminist Companion to Ruth*, The Feminist Companion to the Bible 3 (Sheffield: Sheffield Academic Press, 1993), 142.

9 Beattie, *Targum of Ruth*, 22.

10 Calum M. Carmichael, "A Ceremonial Crux: Removing a Man's Sandal as a Female Gesture of Contempt," *JBL* 96 (1977): 335.

11 Frederic Bush, *Ruth/Esther*, WBC 9 (Dallas: Word Books, 1996), 128.

12 Adele Berlin, *Poetics and Interpretation of Biblical Narrative*, Bible and Literature Series 9 (Sheffield: Almond Press, 1983), 89.

13 For a subversive and deconstructionist reading of Ruth 2, see Danna Nolan Fewell and David Miller Gunn, *Compromising Redemption: Relating Characters in the Book of Ruth*, Literary Currents in Biblical Interpretation (Louisville: Westminster John Knox Press, 1990), 34–45.

14 Sakenfeld, *Ruth*, 48.

CHAPTER FIVE: UNDER GOD'S WINGS

1 Much of what follows is indebted to Dennis T. Olson, *The Death of the Old and the Birth of the New: The Framework of the Book of Numbers and the Pentateuch*, BJS 71 (Chico: Scholars Press, 1985).

2 Thomas W. Mann, *The Book of the Torah: The Narrative Integrity of the Pentateuch* (Atlanta: John Knox Press, 1988), 139.

3 David Atkinson, *The Message of Ruth*, The Bible Speaks Today (Downers Grove, IL: InterVarsity Press, 1991), 67.

4 Martin Kähler, *The So-called Historical Jesus and the Historic Biblical Christ*, trans. Carl E. Braaten, Fortress Texts in Modern Theology (Philadelphia: Fortress Press, 1988), 80, note 11.

5 These comments should not be taken as a denial of infant baptism and noncommunicant membership in the church. God has promised to be the God of his people and their children. The covenant promise and concomitant sign (whether circumcision or baptism) teach that regeneration and a "credible profession of faith" depend on the sovereign grace of the God of Abraham, not on the will of individuals, their parents, or anyone else (John 1:13).

6 Stephen Dray, "Ruth 3:1–4:22: Living in Grace," *Evangel* 14 (1996): 35. This insight calls the postexilic dating of Ruth into question.

Many scholars suggest that Ruth was written to correct the alleged xenophobia of Ezra–Nehemiah. It could be argued that Ezra–Nehemiah and Ruth agree that Israelites could marry Gentiles who professed faith in Yahweh and joined the covenant community. The difference between the two books, regardless of their date, is that Ezra–Nehemiah deals with the problem of intermarriage with unbelieving foreigners and Ruth celebrates Boaz's marriage to a believing foreigner.

7   Murray D. Gow, *The Book of Ruth: Its Structure, Theme and Purpose* (Leicester: Apollos, 1992), 61.

8   Atkinson, *The Message of Ruth*, 73.

9   Edward F. Campbell Jr., *Ruth: A New Translation with Introduction and Commentary*, AB 7 (Garden City, NY: Doubleday, 1975), 112–13.

CHAPTER SIX: OF ALL THAT COULD HAVE GONE WRONG

1   Block, *Judges, Ruth*, 683.

2   Robert L. Hubbard Jr., "Theological Reflections on Naomi's Shrewdness," *TynBul* 40 (1989): 288.

3   Cf. Carmichael, "A Ceremonial Crux," 335; Harold Fisch, "Ruth and the Structure of Covenant History," *VT* 32 (1982): 436; Warren Austin Gage, "Ruth upon the Threshing Floor and the Sin of Gibeah," *WTJ* 51 (1989): 372.

4   Gow, *The Book of Ruth*, 157.

5   Moshe J. Bernstein, "Two Multivalent Readings in the Ruth Narrative," *JSOT* 50 (1991): 19–20; Campbell, *Ruth*, 138.

6   Waldemar Janzen, *Old Testament Ethics: A Paradigmatic Approach* (Louisville: Westminster John Knox Press, 1994), 34.

7   Gage, "Ruth upon the Threshing Floor," 375.

CHAPTER SEVEN: THE BOTTOM LINE

1   Alicia Ostriker, "The Book of Ruth and the Love of the Land," *BibInt* 10 (2002): 356.

2   Wright, *Old Testament Ethics for the People of God*, 55.

3   Jeffrey A. Fager, *Land Tenure and the Biblical Jubilee: Uncovering Hebrew Ethics through the Sociology of Knowledge*, JSOTSup 155 (Sheffield: JSOT Press, 1993), 109–10.

4   Wright, *Old Testament Ethics for the People of God*, 55, 94, 157. See also Keith N. Schoville, "Canaanites and Amorites," in *Peoples of the Old Testament World*, ed. Alfred J. Hoerth, Gerald L. Mattingly, and Edwin M. Yamauchi (Grand Rapids: Baker, 1994), 179.

5   See Ronald J. Leprohon, "Royal Ideology and State Administration in Pharaonic Egypt," in *Civilizations of the Ancient Near East*, ed. Jack M. Sasson (Peabody, MA: Hendrickson, 2000), 286; David O'Connor, "The Social and Economic Organization of Ancient Egyptian Temples," in *Civilizations of the Ancient Near East*, 320; Gösta W. Ahlström, "Adminstration of the State in Canaan and Ancient Israel," in *Civilizations of the Ancient Near East*, 591–92, 598–99.

6   Fager, *Land Tenure and the Biblical Jubilee*, 88. Cf. Sabatino Moscati, *The Face of the Ancient Orient: Near Eastern Civilization in Pre-classical Times* (Mineola, NY: Dover, 2001), 297.

7   Ronald J. Sider, *Just Generosity: A New Vision for Overcoming Poverty in America* (Grand Rapids: Zondervan, 1999), 64.

8   Eryl W. Davies, "Land: Its Rights and Privileges," in *The World of Ancient Israel: Sociological, Anthropological and Political Perspectives*, ed. R. E. Clements (Cambridge: Cambridge University Press, 1989), 361.

9   Sider, *Just Generosity*, 64.

10 See Carol Meyers, "The Family in Early Israel," in *Families in Ancient Israel* (Louisville: Westminster John Knox Press, 1997), 21.

11 Donald A. Leggett, *The Levirate and Goel Institutions in the Old Testament with Special Attention to the Book of Ruth* (Cherry Hill, NJ: Mack Publishing Co., 1974), 19–21.

12 Jeffrey H. Tigay, *Deuteronomy*, JPS Torah Commentary (Philadelphia: Jewish Publication Society, 1996), 482–83.

13 Herbert Chanan Brichto, "Kin, Cult, Land and Afterlife—A Biblical Complex," *HUCA* 44 (1973): 16.

14 I owe this insight to my colleague, Dr. Grant LeMarquand, who is a specialist in African Christianity. Interested readers may wish to consult Michael C. Kirwen, *African Widows* (Maryknoll, NY: Orbis Books, 1979).

CHAPTER EIGHT: MEET MR. SO-AND-SO

1   John P. Baker, "Biblical Attitudes to Romantic Love," *TynBul* 35 (1984): 102.

2   John H. Otwell, *And Sarah Laughed: The Status of Women in the Old Testament* (Philadelphia: Westminster Press, 1977), 143–46; Dean R. Ulrich, "The Framing Function of the Narratives about Zelophehad's Daughters," *JETS* 41 (1998): 529–38.

3   K. Lawson Younger Jr., *Judges/Ruth*, NIVAC (Grand Rapids: Zondervan, 2002), 475–76.

4   Leggett, *The Levirate and Goel Institutions in the Old Testament*, 221.

5   LaCocque, *Ruth*, 112.

6   Block, *Judges, Ruth*, 711.

7   Richard Bauckham, "The Book of Ruth and the Possibility of a Feminist Canonical Hermeneutic," *BibInt* 5 (1997): 35.

8   LaCocque, *Ruth*, 120.

9   Stephen Dray, "Ruth 3:1–4:22: Living in Grace," *Evangel* 14 (1996): 36.

10 Trible, *God and the Rhetoric of Sexuality*, 190.

11 LaCocque, *Ruth*, 108.

12 Davies, "Land: Its Rights and Privileges," 362–63.

13 Leggett, *The Levirate and Goel Institutions in the Old Testament*, 249.

14 LaCocque, *Ruth*, 147.

15 Cf. Gen 2:4; 5:1; 6:9; 10:1; 11:10; 11:27; 25:12; 25:19; 36:1; 36:9.

16 Bruce K. Waltke and Cathi J. Fredricks, *Genesis: A Commentary* (Grand Rapids: Zondervan, 2001), 507–08, 515, 552, 558–59, 567.

CHAPTER NINE: A GLORIOUS PROVIDENCE

1   The inability to conceive, of course, may have had more to do physiologically with the husband than the wife. The Bible does not degrade women who have not been able to become pregnant, but the culture in which the Bible was written may have.

2   Brichto, "Kin, Cult, Land and Afterlife," 22.

3   Cf. Adele Berlin, "Ruth and the Continuity of Israel," in *Reading Ruth*, ed. Judith A. Kates and Gail Twersky Reimer (New York: Ballantine Books, 1994), 259–60.

4   See his *The Book of Isaiah: Chapters 1–39*, NICOT (Grand Rapids: Eerdmans, 1986), and *The Book of Isaiah: Chapters 40–66*, NICOT (Grand Rapids: Eerdmans, 1998).

5 Sakenfeld, *Ruth*, 10.

6 See Joan D. Chittister, *The Story of Ruth: Twelve Moments in Every Woman's Life* (Grand Rapids: Eerdmans, 2000); Marjory Zoet Bankson, *Seasons of Friendship: Naomi and Ruth as a Model of Relationship*, rev. ed. (Minneapolis: Augsburg Fortress, 2005).

7 Tod Linafelt and Timothy K. Beal, *Ruth and Esther* (Collegeville, MN: Liturgical Press, 1999), 81.

POSTSCRIPT

1 Honig's comment that Naomi held Obed because the people of Bethlehem continued to fear Ruth's foreign background and did not think that she could give him a proper upbringing has no foundation in the text. See Honig, "Ruth, the Model Emigrée," 60.

2 Hals, *The Theology of the Book of Ruth*, 7.

3 See Michael V. Fox, *Ecclesiastes*, JPS Bible Commentary (Philadelphia: Jewish Publication Society, 2004), ix–xxxiii; Tremper Longman III, *Ecclesiastes*, NICOT (Grand Rapids: William B. Eerdmans Publishing Company, 1998), 2-40; Leo G. Perdue, *Wisdom and Creation: The Theology of Wisdom Literature* (Nashville: Abingdon Press, 1994), 202-42.

4 Katherine Doob Sakenfeld, *Just Wives? Stories of Power and Survival in the Old Testament and Today* (Louisville: Westminster John Knox Press, 2003), 27-48; "Ruth 4: An Image of Eschatological Hope," in *Liberating Eschatology: Essays in Honor of Letty M. Russell*, ed. M. A. Farley and Serene Jones (Louisville: Westminster John Knox Press, 1999), 60-62; "The Story of Ruth," 215-27.

BIBLIOGRAPHY

Ahlström, Gösta W. "Administration of the State in Canaan and Ancient Israel." In *Civilizations of the Ancient Near East,* ed. Jack M. Sasson, 587–603. Peabody, MA: Hendrickson, 2000.

Atkinson, David. *The Message of Ruth.* The Bible Speaks Today. Downers Grove, IL: InterVarsity Press, 1991.

Baker, John P. "Biblical Attitudes to Romantic Love." *Tyndale Bulletin* 35 (1984): 91–128.

Bankson, Marjory Zoet. *Seasons of Friendship: Naomi and Ruth as a Model of Relationship.* Rev. ed. Minneapolis: Augsburg Fortress, 2005.

Bauckham, Richard. "The Book of Ruth and the Possibility of a Feminist Canonical Hermeneutic." *Biblical Interpretation* 5 (1997): 29–45.

Beattie, D. R. G., trans. *The Targum of Ruth.* Aramaic Bible 19. Collegeville, MN: Liturgical Press, 1994.

Bennett, William J., ed. *The Book of Virtues: A Treasury of Great Moral Stories.* New York: Simon & Schuster, 1993.

Berlin, Adele. *Poetics and Interpretation of Biblical Narrative.* Bible and Literature Series 9. Sheffield: Almond Press, 1983.

———. "Ruth and the Continuity of Israel." In *Reading Ruth,* ed. Judith A. Kates and Gail Twersky Reimer, 255–60. New York: Ballantine Books, 1994.

———. "Ruth: Big Theme, Little Book." *Bible Review* 12 (Aug. 1996): 40–43, 47–48.

Bernstein, Moshe J. "Two Multivalent Readings in the Ruth Narrative." *Journal for the Study of the Old Testament* 50 (1991): 15–26.

Berquist, Jon L. "Role Differentiation in the Book of Ruth." *Journal for the Study of the Old Testament* 57 (1993): 23–37.

Block, Daniel I. *Judges, Ruth*. New American Commentary 6. Nashville: Broadman & Holman, 2002.

Brenner, Athalya. "Naomi and Ruth: Further Reflections." In *A Feminist Companion to Ruth*, 70–84. The Feminist Companion to the Bible 3. Sheffield: Sheffield Academic Press, 1993.

Brettler, Marc Zvi. *The Book of Judges*. Old Testament Readings. London: Routledge, 2002.

Brichto, Herbert Chanan. "Kin, Cult, Land and Afterlife—A Biblical Complex." *Hebrew Union College Annual* 44 (1973): 1–54.

Bright, John. *A History of Israel*. 3rd ed. Philadelphia: Westminster Press, 1981.

Bush, Frederic. *Ruth/Esther*. Word Biblical Commentary 9. Dallas: Word Books, 1996.

Campbell, Edward F., Jr. *Ruth: A New Translation with Introduction and Commentary*. Anchor Bible 7. Garden City, NY: Doubleday, 1975.

Carmichael, Calum M. "A Ceremonial Crux: Removing a Man's Sandal as a Female Gesture of Contempt." *Journal of Biblical Literature* 96 (1977): 321–36.

Chapell, Bryan. *Christ-Centered Preaching: Redeeming the Expository Sermon*. 2nd ed. Grand Rapids: Baker, 2005.

Chittister, Joan D. *The Story of Ruth: Twelve Moments in Every Woman's Life*. Grand Rapids: Eerdmans, 2000.

Davies, Eryl W. "Land: Its Rights and Privileges." In *The World of Ancient Israel: Sociological, Anthropological and Political Perspectives*, ed. R. E. Clements, 349–69. Cambridge: Cambridge University Press, 1989.

Davis, Dale Ralph. *Such a Great Salvation: Expositions of the Book of Judges*. Expositor's Guide to the Historical Books. Grand Rapids: Baker, 1990.

Day, Linda. "Power, Otherness, and Gender in Biblical Short Stories." *Horizons in Biblical Theology* 20 (1998): 109–27.

Dillard, Raymond B., and Tremper Longman III. *An Introduction to the Old Testament*. Grand Rapids: Zondervan, 1994.

Donaldson, Laura E. "The Sign of Orpah: Reading Ruth through Native Eyes." In *Ruth and Esther*, 130–44. A Feminist Companion to the Bible, second series, ed. Athalya Brenner. Sheffield: Sheffield Academic Press, 1999.

Dray, Stephen. "Ruth 3:1–4:22: Living in Grace." *Evangel* 14 (1996): 35–37.

Fager, Jeffrey A. *Land Tenure and the Biblical Jubilee: Uncovering Hebrew Ethics through the Sociology of Knowledge*. Journal for the Study of the Old Testament Supplement Series 155. Sheffield: JSOT Press, 1993.

Fewell, Danna Nolan, and David Miller Gunn. *Compromising Redemption: Relating Characters in the Book of Ruth*. Literary Currents in Biblical Interpretation. Louisville: Westminster John Knox Press, 1990.

———. "'A Son Is Born to Naomi': Literary Allusions and Interpretation in the Book of Ruth." *Journal for the Study of the Old Testament* 40 (1988): 99–108.

Fisch, Harold. "Ruth and the Structure of Covenant History." *Vetus Testamentum* 32 (1982): 425–37.

Fox, Michael V. *Ecclesiastes*. JPS Bible Commentary. Philadelphia: Jewish Publication Society, 2004.

Freedman, Amelia Devin. "Naomi's Experience of God and Its Treatment in the Book of Ruth." *Proceedings of the Eastern Great Lakes and Midwest Biblical Society* 23 (2003): 29–38.

Gage, Warren Austin. "Ruth upon the Threshing Floor and the Sin of Gibeah." *Westminster Theological Journal* 51 (1989): 369–75.

Gow, Murray D. *The Book of Ruth: Its Structure, Theme and Purpose.* Leicester: Apollos, 1992.

Grant, Reg. "Literary Structure in the Book of Ruth." *Bibliotheca Sacra* 148 (1991): 424–441.

Greidanus, Sidney. "Redemptive History and Preaching." *Pro Rege* 19 (1990): 9–18.

Hals, Ronald M. *The Theology of the Book of Ruth.* Philadelphia: Fortress Press, 1969.

Honig, Bonnie. "Ruth, the Model Emigrée: Mourning and the Symbolic Politics of Immigration." In *Ruth and Esther*, 50–74. A Feminist Companion to the Bible, second series, ed. Athalya Brenner. Sheffield: Sheffield Academic Press, 1999.

Howell, James C. "Ruth 1:1–18." *Interpretation* 51 (1997): 281–84.

Hubbard, Robert L., Jr. *The Book of Ruth.* New International Commentary on the Old Testament. Grand Rapids: Eerdmans, 1988.

———. "Theological Reflections on Naomi's Shrewdness." *Tyndale Bulletin* 40 (1989): 283–92.

Janzen, Waldemar. *Old Testament Ethics: A Paradigmatic Approach.* Louisville: Westminster John Knox Press, 1994.

Kähler, Martin. *The So-called Historical Jesus and the Historic Biblical Christ.* Translated by Carl E. Braaten. Fortress Texts in Modern Theology. Philadelphia: Fortress Press, 1988.

King, Greg A. "Ruth 2:1–13." *Interpretation* 52 (1998): 182–84.

Kirwen, Michael C. *African Widows.* Maryknoll, NY: Orbis Books, 1979.

LaCocque, André. *Ruth: A Continental Commentary.* Minneapolis: Fortress Press, 2004.

Leahy, Anthony. "Ethnic Diversity in Ancient Egypt." In *Civilizations of the Ancient Near East*, ed. Jack M. Sasson, 225–34. Peabody, MA: Hendrickson, 2000.

Leggett, Donald A. *The Levirate and Goel Institutions in the Old Testament with Special Attention to the Book of Ruth.* Cherry Hill, NJ: Mack Publishing Co., 1974.

Leprohon, Ronald J. "Royal Ideology and State Administration in Pharaonic Egypt." In *Civilizations of the Ancient Near East*, ed. Jack M. Sasson, 273–87. Peabody, MA: Hendrickson, 2000.

Linafelt, Tod, and Timothy K. Beal. *Ruth and Esther*. Collegeville, MN: Liturgical Press, 1999.

Longman, Tremper, III. *Ecclesiastes*. New International Commentary on the Old Testament. Grand Rapids: Eerdmans, 1998.

Mann, Thomas W. *The Book of the Torah: The Narrative Integrity of the Pentateuch*. Atlanta: John Knox Press, 1988.

Meyers, Carol. "The Family in Early Israel." In *Families in Ancient Israel*, 1–47. Louisville: Westminster John Knox Press, 1997.

Morgenstern, Mira. "Ruth and the Sense of the Self: Midrash and Difference." *Judaism* 48 (1999): 131–45.

Moscati, Sabatino. *The Face of the Ancient Orient: Near Eastern Civilization in Pre-classical Times*. Mineola, NY: Dover, 2001.

O'Connor, David. "The Social and Economic Organization of Ancient Egyptian Temples." In *Civilizations of the Ancient Near East*, ed. Jack M. Sasson, 319–29. Peabody, MA: Hendrickson, 2000.

Olson, Dennis T. *The Death of the Old and the Birth of the New: The Framework of the Book of Numbers and the Pentateuch*. Brown Judaic Studies 71. Chico: Scholars Press, 1985.

Ostriker, Alicia. "The Book of Ruth and the Love of the Land." *Biblical Interpretation* 10 (2002): 343–59.

Oswalt, John N. *The Book of Isaiah: Chapters 1–39*. New International Commentary on the Old Testament. Grand Rapids: Eerdmans, 1986.

———. *The Book of Isaiah: Chapters 40–66*. New International Commentary on the Old Testament. Grand Rapids: Eerdmans, 1998.

Otwell, John H. *And Sarah Laughed: The Status of Women in the Old Testament*. Philadelphia: Westminster Press, 1977.

Ozick, Cynthia. "Ruth." In *A Feminist Companion to Ruth*, ed. Athalya Brenner, 191–214. Sheffield: Sheffield Academic Press, 1993.

Perdue, Leo G. *Wisdom and Creation: The Theology of Wisdom Literature*. Nashville: Abingdon Press, 1994.

Plantinga, Cornelius, Jr. *Not the Way It's Supposed to Be: A Breviary of Sin*. Grand Rapids: Eerdmans, 1995.

Provan, Iain, V. Philips Long, and Tremper Longman III. *A Biblical History of Israel*. Louisville: Westminster John Knox Press, 2003.

Rauber, D. F. "Literary Values in the Bible: The Book of Ruth." *Journal of Biblical Literature* 89 (1970): 27–37.

Sakenfeld, Katharine Doob. *Just Wives? Stories of Power and Survival in the Old Testament and Today*. Louisville: Westminster John Knox Press, 2003.

———. *Ruth*. Interpretation. Louisville: Westminster John Knox Press, 1999.

———. "Ruth 4: An Image of Eschatological Hope." In *Liberating Eschatology: Essays in Honor of Letty M. Russell*, ed. M. A. Farley and Serene Jones, 55–67. Louisville: Westminster John Knox Press, 1999.

———. "The Story of Ruth: Economic Survival." In *Realia Dei: Essays in Archaeology and Biblical Interpretation in Honor of Edward H. Campbell, Jr. at His Retirement*, ed. Prescott H. Williams and Theodore Hiebert, 215–27. Atlanta: Scholars Press, 1999.

Saxegaard, Kristen Moen. "'More than Seven Sons': Ruth as Example of the Good Son." *Scandinavian Journal of the Old Testament* 15 (2001): 257–75.

Schoville, Keith N. "Canaanites and Amorites." In *Peoples of the Old Testament World*, ed. Alfred J. Hoerth, Gerald L. Mattingly, and Edwin M. Yamauchi, 157–82. Grand Rapids: Baker, 1994.

Sider, Ronald J. *Just Generosity: A New Vision for Overcoming Poverty in America*. Grand Rapids: Zondervan, 1999.

Silber, Ursula. "Ruth and Naomi: Two Biblical Figures Revived among Rural Women in Germany." In *Ruth and Esther*, 93–109. A Feminist Companion to the Bible, second series, ed. Athalya Brenner. Sheffield: Sheffield Academic Press, 1999.

Tigay, Jeffrey H. *Deuteronomy*. JPS Torah Commentary. Philadelphia: Jewish Publication Society, 1996.

Trible, Phyllis. *God and the Rhetoric of Sexuality*. Overtures to Biblical Theology. Philadelphia: Fortress Press, 1978.

Tripp, Paul David. *Suffering: Eternity Makes a Difference*. Resources for Changing Lives. Phillipsburg, NJ: P&R Publishing, 2001.

Tull, Patricia K. *Esther and Ruth*. Interpretation Bible Studies. Louisville: Westminster John Knox Press, 2003.

Ulrich, Dean R. "The Framing Function of the Narratives about Zelophehad's Daughters." *Journal of the Evangelical Theological Society* 41 (1998): 529–38.

Vanhoozer, Kevin J. *Is There a Meaning in This Text? The Bible, the Reader, and the Morality of Literary Knowledge*. Grand Rapids: Zondervan, 1998.

Van Wijk-Bos, Johanna W. H. *Ruth and Esther: Women in Alien Lands*. Nashville: Abingdon Press, 2001.

Waltke, Bruce K., and Cathi J. Fredricks. *Genesis: A Commentary*. Grand Rapids: Zondervan, 2001.

Wright, Christopher J. H. *Old Testament Ethics for the People of God*. Downers Grove, IL: InterVarsity Press, 2004.

Younger, K. Lawson, Jr. *Judges/Ruth*. NIV Application Commentary. Grand Rapids: Zondervan, 2002.

INDEX OF SCRIPTURE